THE GIFT OF THE NUTCRACKER

The Gift of the Nutcracker

The Gift of the Nutcracker
978-1-5018-6942-6
978-1-5018-6943-3 eBook
978-1-5018-7614-1 Large Print

The Gift of the Nutcracker / DVD
978-1-5018-6946-4

The Gift of the Nutcracker / Leader Guide
978-1-5018-6944-0
978-1-5018-6945-7 eBook

The Gift of the Nutcracker / Youth Study Book
978-1-5018-6951-8
978-1-5018-6952-5 eBook

The Gift of the Nutcracker / Children's Leader Guide
978-1-5018-7151-1

The Gift of the Nutcracker / Worship Resources
978-1-5018-6953-2 Flash Drive
978-1-5018-6954-9 Download

The Gift of the Nutcracker / Leader Kit
978-1-5018-7618-9

Also by Matt Rawle

The Faith of a Mockingbird
Hollywood Jesus
The Salvation of Doctor Who
The Redemption of Scrooge
What Makes a Hero?

with Juan Huertas and Katie McKay-Simpson

The Marks of Hope: Where the Spirit Is Moving in a Wounded Church

MATT RAWLE

THE GIFT OF THE
Nutcracker

Abingdon Press / Nashville

The Gift of the Nutcracker

Library of Congress Cataloging-in-Publication data has been requested.

978-1-5018-6942-6

18 19 20 21 22 23 24 25 26 27 — 10 9 8 7 6 5 4 3 2 1
MANUFACTURED IN THE UNITED STATES OF AMERICA

To Ken and Kay Irby,
for sharing their ministry
(and many a Christmas) with me.

CONTENTS

INTRODUCTION

Believe it or not, the only member of my family to have danced in *The Nutcracker* is me. Not my daughters, my wife, or my sister. At the age of 19, I donned a toy soldier costume and danced my heart out among all the dolls and snowflakes and mice.

For many families, seeing a performance of *The Nutcracker* is a staple of the Christmas season. Even though the ballet first premiered in Saint Petersburg in 1892, an annual viewing is truly as American as leaving out milk and cookies for Santa. Hundreds of young dancers across the country grace the stage throughout the month of December. The holiday mainstay is so popular that it often pays a dance company's bills for the rest of the year.

What comes to mind when you think of *The Nutcracker*? Perhaps you're reminded of family outings to the ballet to see a sibling or friend dance, or maybe you danced in it yourself and remember the hours of practice and preparation. Do you recall the harrowing battle between the Nutcracker and Mouse King? Or maybe you remember waltzing flowers and dancing candies in the Land of Sweets.

Do you think of Jesus when you ponder the ballet? Probably not. But interestingly enough, the story resonates with strong parallels to Christianity. Stepping back, we can see that Clara represents humanity, perpetually stuck in a stage of waiting. She is cherished by her godfather who gives her the gift of a toy who battles evil, only to be killed in the end and then brought back to life by the godfather himself. After his resurrection, the toy brings Clara to his kingdom, where his subjects have anxiously awaited his return. He greets them all with joy and cheer.

Sound familiar?

The Gift of the Nutcracker explores these Christian themes throughout four chapters, each focusing on a particular character from the story. In turn, each chapter applies the lessons learned from the story to help us better understand our walk as Christians and relationship with Christ.

In Chapter One, "Clara: Waiting for Christmas," we explore the story from our protagonist's point of view. Clara is a young girl at the cusp of adulthood, caught in an "in between" time of life—much like the Advent wait for the coming Christ. She waits to grow up and to be invited to join the adults in their Christmas revelry. Unbeknownst to Clara and to many of us, it is precisely in these periods of waiting that we often see the most growth in our lives.

Chapter Two, "Drosselmeir: A Godfather's Love," focuses on Clara's godfather, who enters the story as a curious figure who doles out odd gifts and acts peculiarly. Sometimes we humans need convincing that something is good, whether it be a Christmas gift under the tree or the gift of Christ himself. We ponder

Drosselmeir's puppet show and wonder how it might foreshadow the story to come. How often does God reveal to us that we need to look forward and navigate the world ahead of us? And how often do we look elsewhere for answers?

Chapter Three, "The Mouse King: Changing Perspective," examines the villain of the Nutcracker story and how much we are influenced by our perceptions. The Mouse King is a mysterious villain and we don't understand his vendetta against the Nutcracker. Clara fears him instinctually. Who wouldn't fear a person-sized mouse? Worry and fear are certainly prevalent in our lives, but just as Clara was comforted with the Nutcracker by her side, we have hope because we know that God will never abandon us.

Chapter Four, "The Nutcracker: The Greatest Gift," is all about good news and seemingly unwanted gifts. The Nutcracker is slain but then resurrected by Clara's godfather, who restores him to his princely form. The Nutcracker Prince then brings Clara back to his kingdom, where they are joyfully met by the masses who have been anticipating their return. It's a happy ending to a story that began with waiting, uncertainty, and a gift that Clara did not even know she wanted or needed.

Much like our journey as Christians, Clara's story is one that begins with uncertainty, fear, and struggle, yet ends with comfort, hope, and joy. Both *The Nutcracker* and the Advent story unfold just as we know they will, but not without the hope and anticipation that always accompany both the dance and the season.

THE POP IN CULTURE

What comes to mind when you hear someone refer to "pop culture"? Do you think of movies and colorful characters or a childhood spent poring over comic book stories? These days, we often associate pop culture with television and the characters and personalities we find there. Pop culture is definitely the home for many of our heroes, both fictional superheroes and the real-life role models we look up to. Many of the stories we want to tell about ourselves are rooted in what we find in our pop-culture accounts.

Regardless of whether you think an example of pop culture is the latest *Superman* comic or something more edgy like *The Walking Dead*, there's no denying that popular music, books, television, movies, and media have much to say about the world in which we live. The word *culture* is used often by many different people in many different ways, but in its simplest form, *culture* is simply an expression of how a community understands itself. God, our Creator, supplies us with the raw ingredients of humanity—talents, time, creativity, desires, ingenuity—and culture is whatever we cook up. Stories, songs, recipes, traditions, art, and language are all displays of how we interpret the world and our place in it.

So what role does God play in our culture—in our day-to-day lives and in the work of our hands, which produces music and art and crafts and literature and plays and movies and technology? Throughout history, people have debated this issue and adamantly drawn a dividing line between that which should be considered *sacred* (that which is explicitly religious in nature) and that which should be considered *secular* (that is, everything else). At first glance, these may seem easy judgments to make, but when we stop to examine what God has to say about this division, we might be surprised at what we find.

Scripture says that all things were made through Christ (John 1:3), and through Christ all things were reconciled to God (Colossians 1:20). In other words, everything and everyone in our world contains a spark of the divine—everything is sacred, and whether or not we choose to live in that truth depends on our perspective. For example, think of sunlight as a holy (sacred) gift from God. God offers us sunlight so we can see the world around us. We can celebrate the sacred by creating things that enhance the light in our homes, such as larger windows or skylights, or we can hang heavy drapes and close the shutters in order to diminish the sacred and shut out the light. Our sacred work is letting in as much light as possible, and those things that keep the light out need to be rejected or transformed. Through Jesus, God put on flesh and walked among us in our world in order to re-narrate what it means to be a child of God.

God assumed culture and transformed it. So now all is sacred, and in everything we are to see and proclaim God's glory. I truly believe we are called not to reject the culture we live in, but to re-narrate its meaning—to tell God's story in the midst of it. Jesus didn't reject the cross (the sin of our world); rather, Jesus accepted it and transformed it from a death instrument into a symbol of life and reconciliation.

Sometimes it's easy to see God in the midst of culture—in the stories of Scripture and in reverent hymns and worshipful icons. Stories of heroes and superheroes often preach the gospel pretty clearly, I think. But other times the divine is more veiled—hidden in a novel, concealed in classic rock, obscured by an impressionist's palate. That is why we created this Pop in Culture series, a collection of studies about faith and popular culture. Each study uses a feature of pop culture as a way to examine questions and issues of the Christian faith. Our hope and prayer is that the studies will open our eyes to the spiritual truths that exist all around us in books, movies, music, and television . . . or even ballet, in this instance.

As we walk with Christ, we discover the divine all around us, and in turn, the world invites us into a deeper picture of its Creator.

Through this lens of God's redemption story, we are invited to look at culture in a new and inviting way. We are invited to dive into the realms of literature, art, and entertainment to explore and discover how God is working in and through us and in the world around us to tell God's great story of redemption.

A Quick Refresher

It's Christmas Eve, and Clara Stahlbaum, her brother, Fritz, and other children are anxiously awaiting their chance to join in on the party their parents are hosting in the parlor. When all of the Christmas preparations are finished, they are finally allowed to come in, where they stare in awe of the beautiful tree lit with what appear to be dozens of stars, decorations made of candy and chocolates, and mounds of presents wrapped in beautifully colored paper. The children are delighted as they open beautiful picture books, fine silk dresses, dutiful and brave toy soldiers, and other wonderful gifts.

Well into the party, a man appears suddenly from the cold, wintry night. He is a mysterious figure wrapped in a cloak, but soon reveals himself to be Clara's godfather, Drosselmeir. He comes bearing delightful gifts to amaze and delight the children. He sets up a puppet theater and tells an exciting tale of a prince and his battle to defeat a wicked mouse. When the puppet show ends, Drosselmeir unveils a new cache of gifts for the children.

Among them are clockwork dolls and also a nutcracker. The intricate clockwork toys Drosselmeir has made mesmerize most of the children, and they overlook the humble nutcracker, who has large eyes and a wide gaping mouth. Clara, however, is drawn to the different toy. She asks what the toy is, and Drosselmeir shows her how to crack nuts in his jaw.

Clara's mischievous brother, Fritz, becomes intrigued by the nutcracker because of Clara's interest and tries to take it from her. In the struggle over the toy, Fritz breaks the toy, much to Clara's dismay, but Drosselmeir promises to repair it before the children are sent off to bed. (In some versions, Fritz breaks the nutcracker's jaw by forcing in a nut that is too big to crack.) Drosselmeir returns with the repaired nutcracker, and Clara gladly goes to bed, relieved that her toy has been restored.

While reflecting on her evening, Clara thinks of all that took place and returns to the parlor to check on the nutcracker. In her sleepy state, she believes she sees Drosselmeir sitting atop their grandfather clock. The clock strikes midnight, and dozens of mice begin running into the room, and the Christmas tree grows to an enormous height. A great puff of smoke appears, and a large, grotesque mouse steps into the room. The Nutcracker also grows to become life-sized, and conflict ensues between the Nutcracker with his army of wooden soldiers and the fiendish Mouse King with his army of mice.

The fighting continues, and it appears the Nutcracker may lose, until Clara distracts the Mouse King by throwing a slipper at him. The Nutcracker is able to defeat the Mouse King and his minions despite his previous injuries. The mice carry off their defeated leader as Clara rushes to the side of the fallen hero. Her godfather, Drosselmeir, reappears, and Clara tearfully asks what can be done to save him. Drosselmeir reaches down and touches the Nutcracker's shoulder. The Nutcracker is transformed into a handsome prince. Clara is overjoyed and thanks her godfather. Drosselmeir tells her that it was her love that saved him. Clara's dress is transformed into a beautiful gown, and the Nutcracker Prince and Clara venture into an enchanted forest sparkling with snow.

On a sleigh pulled by white horses, Clara and the Nutcracker Prince continue on through a magical land to the Land of Sweets, which has been ruled in the Prince's stead by the Sugar Plum Fairy. The Prince tells the Sugar Plum Fairy of his mighty battle and being saved by Clara, which allowed him to transform back into himself. In honor of Clara, the Land of Sweets throws a grand celebration, and desserts from all over the world are gathered for the festivities. There is chocolate from Spain, coffee from Arabia, tea from China, and candy canes from Russia. Shepherdesses from Denmark with strings of flowers perform a waltz to continue the celebration. The Sugar Plum Fairy and her cavalier close the festivities with a dance of their own. The last waltz comes together with all the sweets, and Clara and the Nutcracker Prince leave their thrones to join the dance. As they are dancing, out of the corner of her eye, Clara sees the shadow of Drosselmeir. The music begins to slow and fade, as does the crowd, including her beloved Nutcracker Prince.

Clara suddenly finds herself back in the parlor on the floor with the small, wooden nutcracker toy. She picks up her brave hero, and looks out the window, seeing the magical night she just spent in her dreams.

Chapter One

CLARA: WAITING FOR CHRISTMAS

*We know that the whole creation has been
groaning in labor pains until now.*

Romans 8:22

Christmas seemed to be a magical time of the year when I was a child. Every year my parents invited me to compose a list of what I hoped would appear under the tree. The list detailed what you might expect: the latest toy, the best new video game, a new bike, and branded baseball equipment. The latest and greatest toys and gadgets were gifts I looked forward to with great anticipation, but not everything made it to my list.

Among the wishes for toys and "things," I never listed that I wanted the music on the radio to change to joyful melodies accompanied by sleigh bells. I never wrote down that I hoped the houses in our neighborhood would be glowing with lights. I failed to add my excitement about family coming into town to share a meal and gathering with my church family to sing "Silent Night" by candlelight. Music, lights, family, and worship were left off my list, not because they were unimportant, but because I knew that they would happen. Getting the best baseball helmet on the market was a longshot, but singing with my sisters at the Christmas Eve candlelight service was a blessed given.

What do you hope will happen this Advent and Christmas season? What are you expecting to happen? Which of your traditions seem so certain that writing them down on a wish list seems irrelevant? Many churches welcome the Advent season by lighting candles to welcome Jesus into the world, anticipating the peace, hope, love, and joy Christ continues to offer to us. How might our worship change if we lit a candle giving thanks for peace that we enjoy, rather than what we anticipate in the fulfillment of Isaiah's messianic prophecy—"Nations shall not lift up sword against nation, neither shall they learn war any more" (Isaiah 2:4)? Could it be that one day love will be so prevalent that writing love on a wish list seems irrelevant?

For now, we wait. Like Clara, the one who leads us through this fantastic Nutcracker story, we hope that the gifts under the tree will match the picture of the world in our imagination. We just might discover that the world that awaits is even more grand than what we could ever imagine!

1. THE STAGE IS SET

You're sitting in the audience, and the lights begin to dim. The conductor walks to the podium accompanied with a polite but graceful applause. An oboe offers a steady and crisp "A-440" from which a cacophony of sound slowly erupts, as if something magnificent is awakening. And then…a hint of silence before the baton is lifted and the curtain raised. That pivotal moment between the swell of orchestral chaos and the rising curtain is where the season of Advent lives. Advent, celebrated during the four Sundays prior to Christmas, is a curious season of anticipation for something we know has happened, but has not yet come to fruition. This silent anticipation is a "here and yet not" experience. It's like sitting in the audience for Tchaikovsky's *Nutcracker*. Even if you've never seen the ballet, you most likely have some cultural knowledge of the story. The Sugar Plum Fairy, dancing candies, and toy soldiers have graced the stage since 1892, and yet in that moment before the curtain rises, the show has not begun.

The first Sunday of Advent is the beginning of the Christian New Year, in which the church gathers to hear words from the Hebrew Scriptures that point to a coming Messiah who will fulfill God's promise of everlasting peace and salvation.

> *The days are surely coming, says the* LORD, *when I will fulfill the promise I made to the house of Israel and the house of Judah. In those days and at that time I will cause a righteous Branch to spring up for David; and he shall execute justice and righteousness in the land. In those days Judah will be saved and Jerusalem will live in safety. And this is the name by which it will be called: 'The* LORD *is our righteousness.'*
>
> *Jeremiah 33:14-16*

Scriptures ring out with words of an everlasting kingdom built on foundations of justice, righteousness, safety, and fulfillment. It's easy to see how many understood the Messiah to be an earthly ruler who would establish an independent government, but as the story unfolds in the coming weeks, our worldly expectations are turned upside down, our curiosities piqued.

Curiosity and anticipation go hand in hand. It's like the children in the beginning of the Nutcracker story. Clara, the young girl around whom the story is told, peeks through a keyhole from the family drawing room to see if she can catch sight of what's happening on the other side of the locked door. She can hear the frivolity and catch a fleeting glimpse of dancing, but she can't quite see what she knows is there—the presents under the tree. Presents are a beautiful example of how curiosity and anticipation need each other. A wrapped present under the living room Christmas tree offers a hint of what the gift might be—especially if wrapped creatively, the package suggesting the actual shape of the gift—but because we don't quite know what lies underneath the paper and bow, we are filled with an infectious interest.

Most of us have heard the Christmas story of angels, shepherds, and a silent night, so the Advent anticipation isn't necessarily about how Scripture announces Christ's birth; the anticipation we feel is the curiosity of how God continues to work through Christ from such a humble beginning. It is true that Christ's life, suffering, death, and resurrection confirmed God's promise of an everlasting covenant of eternal life, but there is great work to be done until the world lives in peace, hope, love, and joy. Without a curiosity that calls us into God's continuous work in the world, there is little to anticipate. If you know what gift awaits you under the tree, you aren't holding your breath until Christmas Day. You are certainly thankful for an obvious gift, and most Sundays of the year our worship centers on thanksgiving and praise. Advent is different— our thankfulness is overshadowed by an anticipation born out of curiosity over how a child wrapped in swaddling clothes will save our souls and continue to transform the world.

Clara waits on the other side of the door with a joy she does not yet understand. She's told that the children cannot enter the room until the Christmas tree is lit. I love how light is what invites the children into the party. Light is what invites us into Advent. I remember the first time my wife and I put up a Christmas tree. To say that we added lights to the tree would be an understatement. I lovingly call our first Christmas tree as a married couple "The Bethlehem Supernova." It was like staring into the sun, and my wife couldn't have been more delighted. Since then, the lights on the tree have tapered, but the presence of light hasn't dimmed. We put lights on the tree, on our home, on the mantel, and keep them perpetually burning in the fireplace. The light simply moved from the tree to shine from anything that didn't move!

Light is such an inviting way to welcome the coming light of Christ. In the sanctuary in our church we light candles each week during Advent to light the way, so to speak, on the path to Christmas. This Christmas journey takes us through peace, hope, love, and joy, with the sanctuary lights growing brighter until the entire sanctuary sings "Silent Night" by candlelight. This one, single candle of peace grows to fill the entire sanctuary dancing about in every prayerful hand in much the same way that the light of Christ from a lowly manger grew to change the world. How do you use light in your Christmas decorations? How do you tell Christ's story through light?

In the ballet, once the Christmas tree is lit, the children patiently waiting on the other side of the door are welcomed into the party, and the tree seems larger than life. I remember as a child that the Christmas tree seemed to tower over everything else in the house, but now I can reach the angel at the top with little aid.

Do you remember the tree being larger when you were younger? It's not really about the size of the tree, is it? When I was younger, Christmas meant something different. It was magical and exciting, and nothing else in the world seemed to matter. Today I've grown to realize that it's not about what's under the tree, but those who surround it that matter. Truth be told, this only adds to its magic, excitement, and meaning.

As looming as the tree was for Clara and her friends, it wasn't the tree that had the children's attention. The gifts around the tree held their gaze. Even though the people around the tree are the true gift of Christmas, there's something quite meaningful about giving to others during the Christmas season. I often wonder why we aren't so generous other times of the year. Is it the music, the weather, the end-of-the-year bonus, or do we maybe feel more at peace when Christ is a child? How might we capture that sense of excitement and generosity throughout the year? Maybe it's as simple as continuing a spirit of curiosity and anticipation for God's wonderful and amazing work. My morning prayer most days is "What do you have in store for me today, Lord?" It is an exciting and terrifying thought.

2. IN BETWEEN

The Nutcracker is a story told through the eyes of a twelve-year-old child, and Clara's age offers us a unique perspective on a celebration as meaningful as Christmas. The doorway blocking Clara's entrance into the Christmas party fills her with a sense of anticipation for what lies on the other side, but the doorway represents much more in our story. Clara is on the outside looking in. Being twelve years old, she's no longer a child, but she's not quite an adult, either. She's caught in this "in between" stage of life through which the Nutcracker's story is told. Clara is welcomed into a party with adults, but she's offered a toy as a gift. The gift is precious, something an older child would appreciate, but her younger brother steals it and breaks it. In her dream, she is welcomed into a grand party, but she has to fight off monsters in order to get there. The doorway directly represents a rite of passage between childhood and adolescence.

My oldest daughter is almost twelve years old. On the one hand, she still seems like a child. I see her skipping home from the bus stop in the afternoons after school, she refuses to go upstairs if the lights are off, and convincing her to eat certain vegetables at dinner is an exercise in the art of negotiation. On the other hand, we are living in uncharted parental territory. She texts friends about weekend plans, asks difficult questions that simple answers cannot satisfy, and cares very much about unique fashion trends. She wants privacy, but doesn't want to feel alone. She wants freedom to make her own decisions, but also the security of forgiveness when things don't work out. She wants to sit with her friends during Christmas Eve worship, but she loves when it's just the six of us watching *White Christmas* while Santa's cookies are baking late into the evening. Truth be told, maybe this "in between" stage of life lasts longer than we want to admit.

Maybe this is why The Nutcracker has captured our holiday imagination. Living through this "in between" stage is something we all know on some level, whether we remember the complexity of our own middle school years or have lived through parenting someone in this stage. Being a Christian is an "in between" kind of life. Paul encourages us to "not be conformed to this world, but be transformed by the renewing of your minds" (Romans 12:2). We are citizens of heaven while sojourning on earth. We have one foot in the sanctuary and the other foot in the office. Of course, the kingdom of God is not located in the center of a Venn diagram with heaven on one side and the earth on the other. We can sometimes feel like we are in between worlds, but what we sense as "in between" is actually growth.

The end of Luke 2 offers us a poignant picture of what it looks like to grow within this "in-between" life:

> Now every year his parents went to Jerusalem for the festival of the Passover. And when he was twelve years old, they went up as usual for the festival. When the festival was ended and they started to return, the boy Jesus stayed behind in Jerusalem, but his parents did not know it. Assuming that he was in the group of travelers, they went a day's journey. Then they started to look for him among their relatives and friends. When they did not find him, they returned to Jerusalem to search for him. After three days they found him in the temple, sitting among the teachers, listening to them and asking them questions. And all who heard him were amazed at his understanding and his answers. When his parents saw him they were astonished; and his mother said to him, "Child, why have you treated us like this? Look, your father and I have been searching for you in great anxiety." He said to them, "Why were you searching for me? Did you not know that I must be in my Father's house?" But they did not understand what he said to them. Then he went down with them and came to Nazareth, and was obedient to them. His mother treasured all these things in her heart.
>
> And Jesus increased in wisdom and in years, and in divine and human favor.
>
> *Luke 2:41-52*

Interestingly, the only story we have of Jesus' childhood is when he was twelve. What's more curious is that Luke tells us Jesus grew in wisdom. You might expect that the Messiah was born knowing all that he needed to know about the world, but that's not the story we have. Can you imagine Jesus looking through a keyhole with expectation of what lies on the other side? It certainly gives me a joyful hope that even Jesus used his time on earth to discover and learn about the world. This is also a humbling text for the times I think I have everything figured out.

I've offered a Christmas Eve message for many years, and long before Advent, when I'm planning our Christmas Eve service, I usually sit at the computer with a sense of dread. What am I supposed to say about a text that the congregation has heard so many times that they can recite it from memory? Pastors are often guilty of trying to be witty and enlightening from the pulpit every week instead of simply letting Scripture speak for itself. Surprisingly, every year as we journey closer to celebrating the Nativity, the Holy Spirit always offers me something new to ponder. It fills me with such excitement to offer a new idea every year before singing "Silent Night," but it also gives me a sense of great humility (and even embarrassment) when I look back at previous Christmas Eve sermons and realize how much I didn't truly understand the text as I do in the current moment. This spiritual growth is a joyful humbling that I hope never ceases.

What may be more to the point in Luke's story of Jesus' adolescence is how "in between" isn't either/or, but a both/and. Jesus grew both in wisdom *and* years and in divine *and* human favor. "Wisdom and years" is like the saying that knowledge is knowing a tomato is a fruit, but wisdom is knowing not to put it in a fruit salad. "Human and divine" helps us recognize that Jesus is both fully human and fully divine. As Christians, we don't need to have one foot in the sanctuary and one in the office. The goal is for worship to be productive and the office to be worshipful so that we work to build God's kingdom in all aspects of our lives. When we put both feet in both places, we begin to realize that God's kingdom is always the rock on which we stand.

Seeing the Christmas tree through Clara's twelve-year-old eyes reminds us that being "in between" is always where we find ourselves. By God's grace we are always learning, growing, and being transformed by the renewing of our mind. We are always on one side of a door looking through a keyhole or "in a mirror dimly" (1 Corinthians 13:12). The point is to keep searching, learning, and growing so that one day we will find ourselves complete within the heart of God.

3. TRADITION

Annual Christmas traditions help ground us in our ever-changing, "in between" lives. As crazy as our day-to-day lives can be, we can rest assured of the singing of "Silent Night" by candlelight, opening presents around the tree, and hearing "Jingle Bells" on the radio to the point where we are tired of hearing "Jingle Bells" on the radio. What are some of the traditions you most look forward to each year? Do they happen in the sanctuary or in the living room? Do they involve only your closest loved ones or a large group celebration? Do you long for Christmas Day itself or find more joy in the prior days of preparation?

One of the reasons why Clara is waiting with great expectation to enter into the Christmas party is because she knows what to expect. But not everything goes to plan. One of my favorite Christmas traditions is going to a tree farm to select our perfect tree, and the Advent season two years ago began like any other. We returned home from visiting family for Thanksgiving, quickly unpacked our bags, and headed out to cut down a tree. After selecting our tree and transporting it back to the house on top of a minivan (with no luggage rack, naturally), we dragged it into place. The next morning, we started hanging ornaments. Paper ornaments were placed on the bottom (the ones within toddler reach), and glass decorations adorned the top. The tree is always a beautiful and well-designed centerpiece of our living room. Later that afternoon I left to attend a church council meeting to approve the next year's budget ('tis the season), and my wife called me in a panic. The tree wasn't as secure as we had thought, and it had toppled over, breaking all of our glass ornaments. It may not seem like a tragedy with a wide-angle lens, but in the moment, it was heartbreaking. Our ornaments aren't just thoughtless items purchased willy-nilly and randomly placed on the tree for a family photo—the tree tells our family's story. Ornaments we had inherited from family, gifts we had received from friends, and mementos purchased through the years were all in a shattered mess on the floor. It seemed that part of our story was gone. Traditions keep us grounded, but sometimes the ground shifts.

When Clara enters the party her godfather, Drosselmeir, offers her a special gift. It seems that her Christmas party expectations were exceeded. Not long after receiving her gift, her brother, Fritz, tries to wrestle the toy away from her, breaking it in the process. The joy of her fulfilled expectations is quickly dashed. Have you ever experienced unmet expectations, or looked forward to something only to watch it go horribly wrong? Of course you have—it's part of the human experience. In these moments, sometimes we feel panic or fear. Other times we may become angry in our disappointment. And sometimes when things go wrong we even discover a new, more helpful perspective.

Let's return to twelve-year-old Jesus in the Temple (Luke 2). Every year Jesus' family went up to Jerusalem to celebrate the Passover, but when Jesus turned twelve, the long-standing tradition changed. During the trip home Jesus' family realized that Jesus wasn't with them.

Mary and Joseph rushed back to the Temple to find Jesus listening to the teachers and asking them questions. Mary said, "Child, why have you treated us like this? Look, your father and I have been searching for you in great anxiety," which I think is the censored version of her response. When things don't go according to plan, anxiety can take over. Our minds begin to race. We start thinking of the best of what the past had to offer and the worst of what an uncertain future might present, and anxiety is the glue that holds them together. Jesus replied, "Did you not know that I must be in my Father's house?" Obviously not, Jesus. Scripture says that they did not understand what Jesus was saying.

Advent rests in the tension-filled space between Jesus' birth and his continuous work that propels us into the future. In a way, Advent is always. Much like Mary and Joseph, this can fill us with anxiety and uncertainty. The good news is that Christ is perpetually found in the center. We often light the candle of peace on the first Sunday of Advent to remind us that being in Christ is not about having all of the answers; rather welcoming Christ into our life is about being at peace with ourselves, God's world, and a future that we often wish we could predict.

We like to think that our traditions never change, but that's not true. I would love to say that our traditions are the constant of Christmas, but as the saying goes, the only true constant is change. Our Christmas traditions might slowly evolve over many years, or you might find them in a shattered and unexpected mess on the floor. What we eventually discovered when our tree toppled over is that the ornaments on the tree were not nearly as important as the people who gather around it or the reason we gather in the first place. When Clara's surprise gift is broken, it seems that the Christmas party was all for nothing, but Drosselmeir has one more surprise to offer. He takes the nutcracker and mends it as if it had never been broken. What we discover in this tug of war between Clara and Fritz is that the real gift that night was not the nutcracker itself, but the person who offered the gift. In other words, it's not singing "Silent Night" that holds our Christmas together, it is the One of whom we sing who provides the meaning. I guess you could say that the only thing constant is change, but our traditions reveal that the constant is Christ himself.

4. MIDNIGHT

After all the guests had left, Clara got into bed, but she found it hard to fall asleep. She couldn't stop thinking about the Christmas tree, the toys, and most of all, the curious nutcracker her godfather had given her. I love waking up on the 25th, but I hate having to close my eyes on the 24th. I know that in the morning my children will wake up and open their gifts, and memories will be made for good or ill. I know that Jesus said, "So do not worry about tomorrow, for tomorrow will bring worries of its own. Today's trouble is enough for today" (Matthew 6:34), but sometimes it's hard to close your eyes knowing that tomorrow will have problems of its own.

The story of Jesus' birth sounds like a story about sleepless nights. Before Joseph and Mary were married, Mary was pregnant. Scripture doesn't reveal the conversations Mary and Joseph had with each other when this scandal was discovered. As a pastor, I really wish I could have been a fly on the wall to overhear how this young couple, steeped in faith, were able to navigate such news. To further complicate matters, Mary is silent throughout Matthew's Gospel. In Luke's account, Joseph doesn't say anything. In fact, we don't have any recorded conversations between the two at all.

The Gospel of Luke tells us that Mary knew what God was planning. The angel Gabriel appears before her and says:

> *"Do not be afraid, Mary, for you have found favor with God. And now, you will conceive in your womb and bear a son, and you will name him Jesus. He will be great, and will be called the Son of the Most High, and the Lord God will give to him the throne of his ancestor David. He will reign over the house of Jacob forever, and of his kingdom there will be no end."*
>
> *Luke 1:30-33*

What may be even more impressive than the angel's proclamation is Mary's answer: "Let it be with me according to your word" (Luke 1:38b). We aren't told why Mary greeted God's word with affirmation. Was her voice shaking with fear? Was her answer brief because awe and wonder had overcome her? Did she see the angel through tears of joy for what God was doing? We don't know, but we can be relatively sure that a peaceful sleep is not what followed. What would Joseph think? Was the angel going to Joseph as well, and if not, how was Mary supposed to tell him? The Gospel of Luke doesn't tell us any of that either.

Matthew's Gospel tells us about Jesus' birth through Joseph's perspective, and the news is more surprising than what Luke remembered. Mary "was found to be with child from the Holy Spirit" (Matthew 1:18b). Scripture tells us, "For surely I know the plans I have for you" (Jeremiah 29:11a), and I'm sure that Joseph would have appreciated God revealing this plan in a less surprising way. One of my clergy friends often says that God's middle name is Surprise, but I'm beginning to believe that God's middle name is Suspense. It's like when Abraham has brought his son Isaac up the mountain to sacrifice him to the Lord. Just as the knife is in Abraham's hand, an angel swoops in to stop the slaughter. Moses and the ancient Israelites are standing between the waters of the sea and Pharaoh's chariots, causing the people to scream out in terror, but then the waters part, offering them a pathway to freedom. When Jesus hears that his friend Lazarus is at the point of death, Jesus waits for two days before traveling to Bethany.

Does God purposefully wait until the last moment to intervene in these stories? After Clara falls asleep, she finds herself in an unexpected place. She begins to dream, but her dream quickly becomes a nightmare. Mice twice her size come out of nowhere with swords at the ready. The Nutcracker springs to life surrounded by soldiers equipped to save the day. From Clara's perspective, the Nutcracker comes to her defense at the last moment, but I wonder if she was so focused on the mice closing in on her that she missed that the Nutcracker was there the whole time.

Could it be that Abraham was too preoccupied to notice the ram caught in the thicket? Were the Israelites so focused on Egypt that they couldn't see that the winds were already pushing back the waves? How often do we focus on what's going wrong so much that we fail to notice God's activity in what's going right?

Could it be that Abraham was too preoccupied to notice the ram caught in the thicket? Were the Israelites so focused on Egypt that they couldn't see that the winds were already pushing back the waves? How often do we focus on what's going wrong so much that we fail to notice God's activity in what's going right? God's timing is one among many questions I hope to ask in heaven one day.

I remember one evening when my oldest daughter was having trouble breathing because of whooping cough. I spent the night with her alternating between sitting outside in the cold air and holding her in the shower steam of the hallway bathroom. She slept well when her breathing became easier, but I certainly didn't. I remember holding her late into the next morning wondering how many sleepless nights Mary and Joseph must have had. How many sleepless nights does God have while watching humanity run amok?

Have you ever had a sleepless night? Was it excitement that kept you awake, or maybe fear or worry that made it impossible to close your eyes? Were you able to find enough peace to fall asleep or did your body concede simply out of exhaustion? I remember visiting a family in the hospital after a terrible car accident that left a mother and her four-year-old daughter in critical condition. Every moment mattered. No one slept a wink. The mere suggestion of sleep seemed almost offensive. After two weeks of 24-hour-a-day monitoring, the young girl died. I haven't cried with a family that hard in a long time. I thought the trauma, along with constant wakefulness, might destroy this young family's faith, but I couldn't have been more wrong. Certainly, there will be difficult times ahead for this precious family, but the genuine faith they have in God and in one another left me in a reverent silence. Maybe that's why Mary is silent in Matthew, and Joseph is silent in Luke: the faith of the other was enough.

When Clara has the spotlight in our story, the Nutcracker stands in the wings, and when the Nutcracker has all of the action, Clara simply observes. There is an artful humility in knowing where the spotlight needs to be. If the light becomes pointed on us during the Advent and Christmas season, we might forget that Christ is the one who is the light of the world. If we hold the spotlight, we might miss the ram in the thicket and the waters parting.

5. IS THIS REAL?

Clara rubs her eyes in disbelief. Is she dreaming? Is this really happening? Does it matter? Have you ever been in a situation that defies belief? Have you ever found yourself in a place that didn't seem real? Many times I've been with people in emergency room waiting rooms just thinking that if they could wake up, this terrible nightmare would be over. I've also been witness to "pinch-me-I-must-be-dreaming" moments of unspeakable joy.

I remember when my wife and I were first-time parents, and so much of those first few months just didn't seem real. We had just moved back to Louisiana after seminary, so we were in a new town, were new to the life of a pastor, and we were new parents. The long nights, the crying that comes out of nowhere, and the constant attention required to care for a new baby (or did you think I was talking about the church?) had us questioning our sanity. In mid-November of that year I had a chance to preach in the contemporary service. I was so exhausted from everything that was happening in my life that this sermon will likely go down in history as the worst sermon I have ever given (though there's still time).

On paper the sermon was fine enough, but once I gave it a title and artwork, everything started to unravel. It was called, "Han

Solo Wouldn't Say I Love You." It was supposed to be about how Harrison Ford knew his character so well that when the *Empire Strikes Back* script called for him to respond to Princess Leah's "I love you" with "I love you, too," he knew to improvise with the famous "I know." This was supposed to be a model for how we are to know our Christian character so well that we can improvise when life offers the unexpected, but it was a total disaster. Halfway through the sermon, I began to stray from the manuscript, which is a pretty regular occurrence, but I couldn't remember how to find my way back. I literally forgot what I was talking about and couldn't find my place to get back to the message. I panicked, looked up at the congregation, apologized, and simply said, "Amen."

It was a total nightmare, being only four months out of seminary. I just ended the sermon right there. There was no eloquent tie-in to the first paragraph. There was no convicting action step to lead the congregation out into the world. There wasn't even a clever question for the church to ponder in the coming week. I just... stopped. It is ironic that the sermon was about the ability to improvise in the midst of the unexpected, and when faced with the unexpected, I totally broke. It almost didn't seem real.

Back to the ballet. Clara rubbed her eyes in disbelief when she found herself surrounded by what seemed to be a great and unexpected threat. Curiously, the clock strikes twelve in the background. Does this mean she isn't dreaming after all? It makes me think of the angels appearing before the shepherds in the fields keeping watch over their flocks to announce Jesus' birth. It certainly was an unbelievable sight, which is why the angel says, "This will be a sign for you: you will find a child wrapped in bands of cloth and lying in a manger" (Luke 2:12). Sometimes we need a sign. We need affirmation. When the Holy Spirit inspires us to take risks, to pick up the cross, and to step out in faith, God will always supply a sign, a touchstone, or something tangible to affirm our conviction.

Although God offers affirmation, we must certainly take care in assigning meaning to occurrences and interpreting signs. I heard a story once about a man who was torn between staying in town and remaining in his current job or moving halfway across the country to start something new. He prayed that God might show him which way he ought to go. One morning while having his coffee he saw a cardinal land on his fence. After a moment or two the cardinal flew away. The man saw this as a sign that he was to move and start a new job. Was that God sending a message? Or did the man truly want to move and reach to find a sign in a simple occurrence in nature?

Seeing signs in nature or taking coincidences out of context can be a dangerous way to do theology. Often people will ask me to help them make a decision. I always ask if they've prayed about what God is calling them to do. If they still are unsure, I offer something simple. I take out a coin and say, "If it comes up heads, do this. If it comes us tails, do this." I flip the coin, reveal how it fell, and then check their reaction. Whether they are relieved or concerned by how the coin flipped reveals that they have already made their decision. Most of the time, people simply want assurance that their decision is correct. Let me be clear that flipping a coin is a terrible way to make a life-changing decision. The point is that we aren't as torn as we think we are. After showing them that they do know what they feel called to do, I then ask them to search for Christ in their decision.

We pray for discernment, and then we look for Christ. We sometimes flip a coin if we have to, but the affirmation God always supplies is the presence of Christ.

We pray for discernment, and then we look for Christ. We sometimes flip a coin if we have to, but the affirmation God always supplies is the presence of Christ.

Whether or not the towering mice are real is beside the point. When Clara rubs her eyes with doubt is when the clock chimes midnight and the Nutcracker wakes up.

Sometimes when we doubt is when we see Christ most clearly. I don't mean doubt as the opposite of faith or being faithful; rather doubt as the awareness that we don't have all of the answers. Sometimes we think that when we are faithful disciples of Jesus Christ, our lives become mapped out with all of the answers, and we just apply a holy checklist accordingly. When this is the case, we become deaf to any idea that isn't our own. We can become prideful and haughty. We begin dangerously to think that God is on our side and not with our neighbor, as if God can't be in two places at once. Of course, being a disciple means we live disciplined lives, but even Mary asked Gabriel, "How can this be?" When we are brave enough to ask, Christ is always revealed. When Clara felt hopeless is when the Nutcracker became real.

Devotion

A DIFFERENT KIND OF WAITING

And now, O Lord, what do I wait for?
My hope is in you.

Psalm 39:7

"Look, the virgin shall conceive and
bear a son,
and they shall name him
Emmanuel,"

which means, "God is with us."

Matthew 1:23

Advent is a season of waiting. Most of us do not enjoy times of waiting but do everything we can to avoid or abbreviate them. Our "instant everything" culture gives ample evidence of our impatience. Whether it's waiting in traffic, waiting in line, waiting for a reply to a text message, or waiting for a test result, we view these times as inconveniences and aggravations. Yet Advent is a different kind of waiting.

The word "Advent" comes from the Latin word *adventus,* meaning an "arrival" or "coming." During Advent we eagerly anticipate the celebration of the birth of Christ, as well as look forward to his glorious return. Unlike other times of waiting, this waiting is marked not

THE GIFT OF THE NUTCRACKER

by anxiety or dread but by joy-filled expectation. Just as Clara and the other children excitedly waited for the signal that the Christmas tree had been lit and they could enter the room where they would find special gifts chosen just for them, we wait in Advent with eager and confident expectation knowing that Christ has come. God is with us. This is the message of Christmas, and it can transform all of our waiting.

What are you waiting for at this time in your life? What uncertainty are you facing? Whatever it may be, remember that you are not alone. Recognizing and welcoming Christ's presence enables us to wait with expectancy, knowing that the gifts of hope, peace, and joy can be ours regardless of our circumstances.

God of hope, thank you for sending your Son into the world—Emmanuel, God with us. In this season of waiting, I pray for eyes to see and experience the presence and light of Christ all around me and within me. Amen.

Chapter Two

DROSSELMEIR:
A GODFATHER'S LOVE

The LORD is my light and my salvation;
whom shall I fear?
The LORD is the stronghold of my life;
of whom shall I be afraid?
                    —Psalm 27:1

I vividly remember the birth of my first child. I went with my wife for what we thought was a routine doctor visit. The doctor took one look and sent us directly across the street to register at the hospital. Thank goodness we had a bag packed in the back seat of the car. The next few hours were filled with excitement as we called family and friends to let them know of the new timeline. We arrived at the hospital in the middle of the night, and little did I know that this would be the first of many sleepless nights.

My mother arrived early the next morning, after I'd had a very long evening of pacing the floor and watching the monitors. In a daze, I asked her when she started sleeping normally again after I was born. She asked me how old I was. "I'm 28," I answered. She quickly replied, "Then it's been at least 28 years since I've had a good night's sleep." Now that my oldest is ten years old, my mother's quick-witted answer is proving to be more prophecy than timely comic banter.

When we read about Jesus' birth, we hear glorious words from angels and shepherds. We get an inside view on Joseph's dreams. We hear that Mary treasured and pondered the experience in her heart. It seems that the only person who remains silent on a not-so-silent night is God. Have you ever imagined what God was thinking during the first Christmas? We might think that God knows everything, but if we dig deep into Scripture, we see that this isn't always the case. When Abraham offers Isaac as a sacrifice, the angel of the Lord swoops down and says, "Do not lay a hand on the boy or do anything to him; for now I know that you fear God, since you have not withheld your son, your only son, from me" (Genesis 22:12). God seems surprised when Israel turns away in Jeremiah 3:7, and indecisive with Israel in the wilderness in Exodus 33:5. Though stories about God being surprised are few, there still exists a space for the unexpected.

Was God pacing the floor of the heavenly firmaments until hearing Jesus' first cry? Was God hoping the shepherds would find their way to Bethlehem? Did God know that Joseph's dream would compel him not to dismiss Mary when she was found to be with child? Does God know what it's like to hold your breath in anticipation? All of these questions may remain a mystery, which may be why Drosselmeir is such a mysterious figure in Clara's story. Drosselmeir is Clara's godfather. He offers toys, performs a puppet show, and mends broken things, but he is much more than a Santa Claus offering gifts on a snowy, winter's evening. What might this mysterious character reveal about the character of God?

1. FIRST IMPRESSIONS

Have you ever received a Christmas present that wasn't exactly what you'd hoped for? I remember all the times I received practical gifts like socks or savings bonds from relatives. I received those gifts with an obligatory "thank you" and was very disappointed in their lack of flashiness or play time. Now that I'm an adult, of course I've changed my mind (I do love a good pair of socks). First impressions are not always final impressions.

In *The Nutcracker* story, not long after the children are filled with Christmas excitement, the party comes to a standstill. The door flings open to reveal a cloaked figure accompanied by a chill in the air and silence in the room. In that moment, their delight turned to dread. It's like the year my nephew received a toy tiger as a gift. A bright, excited smile danced on his face when he first opened the present. When he touched the tiger's back, however, it started to walk and roar, startling him and turning that gleeful smile into tears instantaneously.

It doesn't take much for frivolity to become fear, which is why we light a candle of peace during Advent. The Israelites had been exiled to Babylon in the sixth century BC, and their future, their story, and their identity as God's people appeared to be in jeopardy. Upon their return, God offered beautiful words of comfort and hope recorded in the Book of Isaiah:

Comfort, O comfort my people,
   says your God.
Speak tenderly to Jerusalem,
   and cry to her
that she has served her term,
   that her penalty is paid,
that she has received from the LORD's *hand*
   double for all her sins.

A voice cries out:
"In the wilderness prepare the way of the LORD,
   make straight in the desert a highway for
   our God.
Every valley shall be lifted up,
   and every mountain and hill be made low;
the uneven ground shall become level,
   and the rough places a plain.
Then the glory of the LORD *shall be revealed,*
   and all people shall see it together,
   for the mouth of the LORD *has spoken."*
                                   Isaiah 40:1-5

Not only does the Lord's word offer assurance of God's presence and a hope for the future, but it is also our example of how God desires us to respond in times of great tragedy and grief. In *The Nutcracker*, when the cloaked figure enters the room, the children's Christmas anticipation and joy disappear, seemingly impossible to recover. Clara runs to her father's side to seek comfort, as God hopes we might in times of great fear.

After God calls for comfort, there is a voice that cries out—"In the wilderness prepare the way of the LORD, make straight in the desert a highway for our God" (Isaiah 40:3). We do not know whose voice it is, or from where it comes, but it carries a powerful word. This proclamation not only reveals a deep and profound truth about God, but it also reveals that God is moving. First, this word begins with location. It does not say "In the land of plenty, prepare for the Lord," or "Safely in your living room prepare for the Lord," or "In the line at the department store prepare for the Lord." *In the wilderness* is where God is moving. It is that desolate place where life seems absent and nourishment difficult to find, and where pathways change as quickly as the wind blows. This is where God chooses to move. When we meditate on the coming of the Christ, we should not expect to be comfortable. When the Holy Spirit starts to move for angels to sing and the shepherds to run and the wise men to follow a star, it is far from a silent night.

We light the candle of peace because we have to. When God appears, it is not an accident that God offers a word of comfort through messengers saying, "Be not afraid." The valleys are lifted up and the mountains made low. The uneven ground will be made level and the rough places plain. We light the candle of peace because without it we might be terrified by the quaking ground. We hold on to peace because if we don't, we might beat our plowshares into swords and resist out of fear. God is traveling down a highway through the wilderness, but if we are frightened by the storm that the Incarnation has presented to the powers and mighty of the world, we might just think the wilderness is where we are supposed to stay.

Secondly, the voice crying out offers a command: "In the wilderness *prepare* the way of the LORD." Instead of beating our plowshares into swords out of fear, we are to use them to clear the path. How do you think the mountains are lowered and the valleys are lifted up? It is not by lightning bolts, but by human hands inspired by God's awesome presence. We prepare the way of the Lord by recognizing that the mountains are peaks that we have built to claim that some are more powerful than others. The valleys are places we have dug to offer a pit for those we think are unworthy. This highway is not a place of grayness where all are the same and there is no diversity; rather it is a place where we recognize that the way things are is not the way things have to be, and when the work is done, then we shall see the glory of God.

Finally, there is a relationship change that happens between the beginning and the end of the text. In the beginning, we hear, "Comfort, O comfort my people, says your God." In a way, it seems that God is being reintroduced to God's people. This is *your* God. The Lord is the one who created the foundations of the world, the one who brought you out of Egypt, the one who journeyed with you into exile, and the one who offers you comfort now for the return home. "Comfort," says *your* God. But then when we make straight a highway, *your* God becomes *our* God. At first we might need convincing.

Sometimes when we look at the world, God can seem dramatically absent, or at least, not the ever-present God we imagined. But then, when we come together to raze the mountains and raise the valleys, God is our God and has always been our God. Whether we are walking in the garden, making bricks without straw, building a temple in which to worship, or turning away when the temple crumbles. It's like when the angel Gabriel appears before Mary to say, "Do not be afraid, Mary, for you have found favor with God. And now, you will conceive in your womb and bear a son, and you will name him Jesus." Mary replies with, "How can this be?" (Luke 1:26-38). It is a "your God" kind of moment. But before the angel departs, Mary replies, "Here am I, the servant of the Lord." It becomes an "Our God" moment.

The journey begins with peace. Peace is not lack of conflict in the world. Following Christ means turning over the money-changing tables, speaking truth to power, feeding the hungry even when your finance team thinks it's too expensive, and making decisions that are better for your soul than your popularity. The kind of peace Christ ushers into the world is not a lack of conflict; a Kingdom peace is a lack of violence. Think about the Christmas Truce of 1914, in which French, German, and British troops in the midst of World War I put their weapons down to exchange food, trade prisoners, and join together in carol-singing on Christmas Eve. This brief moment of peace was nothing less than a miracle. The difficult news is that when the singing was over, so was the peace. So we light the candle of peace to remind ourselves that we should be at peace all 365 days of the year.

The journey begins with peace. Peace is not lack of conflict in the world. Following Christ means turning over the money-changing tables, speaking truth to power, feeding the hungry even when your finance team thinks it's too expensive, and making decisions that are better for your soul than your popularity.

---

2. PUPPETS AND PROPHECY

The great and mysterious figure in *The Nutcracker* removes his cloak to reveal that he is Clara's godfather, Drosselmeir. The children's fear melts away as quickly as his smile is broad. Drosselmeir is a well-loved man in the community, and the children know that they are in for a treat. He offers them a surprise puppet show full of adventure, peril, and a wonderfully happy ending. A small marionette prince and princess walk across the stage interrupted by a mouse king blocking their way. The prince and the Mouse King draw swords in a dance of good vs. evil. The Mouse King is vanquished, and the princess is saved. Good prevails as victor.

The audience doesn't know that this puppet show reveals nearly everything we need to know about the rest of the story. It seems insignificant if you're seeing the story unfold for the first time, but for those of us who know the story, it makes total sense. During the season of Advent, we often read scriptures that point to Jesus being the long-promised Messiah. Because we in the church know how the story ends, it makes great sense to gather the choir and sing, "His name shall be called Wonderful Counselor, Almighty God, Everlasting Father, the Prince of Peace," which Handel immortalized in his *Messiah* oratorio. If we were living in the first century, it would hardly seem appropriate to recognize a child wrapped in swaddling clothes lying in a manger as the Almighty God and Everlasting Father.

God has spoken with humanity through burning bushes, mountaintop experiences, and voices from heaven, but most of the time God seems to use a messenger to get the point across. God's words through the prophets point to the way things are, the way things should be, and a future promise. Sometimes we think that prophecy is like biblical fortune telling, that regardless of our actions, God will do what was planned, but biblical prophecy is quite the opposite. Prophecy calls attention to current actions and where those current actions will lead. It's like the auto repair shop I recently visited. The mechanic told me that I needed to replace the timing belt, and if I hadn't come in that day, soon the belt would have broken, causing lots of expensive damage. It's not that the mechanic could see into the future, but the mechanic knows cars well enough to know what will happen if repairs aren't made. It's not that God's prophets announce the future like a holy fortune cookie, but God knows God's creation well enough to know the future result of current actions.

Drosselmeir's puppet show provides general foreshadowing, but it's not specific enough to spoil the story. The Old Testament prophecies we read during Advent offer us a snapshot of who God's Messiah will be, but Scripture doesn't offer a day or time for the Messiah's arrival. On the one hand, this means that prophesies such as "O Bethlehem...from you shall come forth for me one who is to rule in Israel...from ancient days" (Micah 5:2), "out of Egypt I called my son" (Hosea 11:1), and "Look, the young woman is with child and shall bear a son, and shall name him Immanuel" (Isaiah 7:14) need interpretation. As Christians, we read all Scripture through the lens of the Trinity, meaning that Scripture is the story of the Father, Son, and Holy Spirit all at work as one divine Lord. Two thousand years' worth of interpretation makes these prophesies clear, but we can see how many during Jesus' lifetime were suspicious of "Joseph's boy" preaching with such authority (Luke 4:22).

On the other hand, these prophecies are vague because God knows us well. It's like when the disciples asked Jesus when the end of the world might be—

> Jesus answered them, "Beware that no one leads you astray. For many will come in my name, saying, 'I am the Messiah!' and they will lead many astray. And you will hear of wars and rumors of wars; see that you are not alarmed; for this must take place, but the end is not yet. For nation will rise against nation, and kingdom against kingdom, and there will be famines and earthquakes in various places: all this is but the beginning of the birth pangs."
>
> Matthew 24:4-8

Jesus first says that many will claim to be the Messiah. Had the Old Testament prophecies been specific, how many would have used this to their advantage for power and authority? Maybe more to the point—we should always be ready for Christ's return. If we knew that Christ was returning on Tuesday, then our sanctuaries wouldn't be full until Monday. The Old Testament prophecies show us that the Messiah is a suffering servant with great authority born in one of the least of towns with peace as his title. Humility, peace, lowliness, and authority are markers that God's heart is being revealed.

These prophecies and readings have a vagueness about them for all the right reasons. It's like the afternoon that someone came into my office asking me if I thought the recent solar eclipse was a sign of Christ's return. I asked him what he might do if it were a sign. He said that he would return to church to "get right" with the Lord. I asked what he might do if the eclipse wasn't a sign of Christ's return. He replied with, "I guess I would keep looking." I invited him to start his looking with us in our church. Unfortunately, I don't think he was impressed with my answer.

Drosselmeir's puppet show offered the children an idea of what was about to unfold, but it didn't reveal everything. Otherwise there would be little reason for the story to continue.

Scripture doesn't tell us everything we want to know, but it does reveal everything we need. During the Advent season, we wait for the one who reveals God's heart through humility, suffering, peace, and authority.

Scripture doesn't tell us everything we want to know, but it does reveal everything we need. During the Advent season, we wait for the one who reveals God's heart through humility, suffering, peace, and authority.

3. GOOD GIFT OR BAD GIFT?

The puppet show isn't Drosselmeir's only surprise. After the puppet show concludes, Drosselmeir offers additional toys for the children. A ballerina, a clown, and a fairy dance about as if they are alive. The show that was behind the curtain springs to life and enters into the real world. The story is becoming real, and as Clara will soon discover, this is only the beginning.

God's story becoming real in our life is what the Christmas story is about. In a way, the prophecies about the coming Messiah become so full of God's Holy Spirit that they come alive in the person of Jesus Christ. But the Incarnation means little if we do not incorporate Christ into our daily lives. It's like leaving a gift under the tree unopened. If we don't receive the gift, open it up and use it, it's as if the gift wasn't offered in the first place.

As a United Methodist, when I talk about connecting with God through Christ, I use the word *grace*. Grace is God's gift, and we can think about this gift in three distinct ways. First, grace is a gift offered. There's something under the tree waiting for you even before you know to look for it. This gift is not earned or deserved. It is freely offered to all without price. God's Prevenient Grace, divine love that moves toward us before we move toward God, is a gift to humanity that humanity doesn't know it needs.

Second, God's grace is also a gift received and accepted. My daughters love playing "Santa" Christmas morning, searching under the tree, checking labels to see which gift goes to whom.

We always take time to watch everyone open gifts individually, so that we can celebrate what everyone has received. I haven't yet experienced someone rejecting a Christmas present. I bet God wishes the same kind of acceptance to the divine gift of salvation. I love how the language of baptism speaks to God's grace as a gift received. "Do you accept the freedom and power God gives you to resist evil, injustice, and oppression in whatever forms they present themselves?"[1] is one of the questions we ask when someone comes forward for baptism in my congregation. Before we ask new Christians if they confess Jesus Christ as their Lord and savior, we first ask if they accept the freedom and power to resist. There is power in knowing that we rest in God's grace and in the knowledge that there are no hoops through which we have to jump to be loved by God. This is Justifying Grace.

Resisting, the art of saying no, is an important discipline in the church. The problem lies in saying no to the wrong things. Every "no" you give is a "yes" to something else, and vice versa. If I say "yes" to a late-night meeting at the church, I am also saying "no" to helping my kids with their homework that evening. If I say "yes" to taking a Sabbath from the office, I am saying "no" to whatever non-emergencies cross my e-mail inbox. More to the point, if I allow gossip in hallway conversations, or let a racial slur go unchallenged, I am saying "no" to my baptismal vow. God offers us freedom and power to "resist evil, injustice, and oppression in whatever forms they present themselves." There is freedom in the sense that we have to use judgment and discernment. Evil would be easy to resist if it were obvious.

I don't always get this right, and neither does my neighbor. This is why grace is also an ongoing experience of being continually transformed (Sanctifying Grace). There is this troublesome verse in Matthew 6—"For if you forgive others their trespasses, your heavenly Father will also forgive you; but if you do not forgive others, neither will your Father forgive your trespasses" (Matthew 6:14-15). This goes into the category of Things I Wish Jesus Hadn't Said. I wish Jesus' words were about what God has done for us, that everything is covered, and I don't have to worry about how I am treating my neighbor or my enemy.

This is why in the United Methodist Church we talk about grace as being Prevenient, Justifying, and Sanctifying. The gift is under the tree ready and waiting for you. The gift must be received and opened, unwrapped and investigated. Finally, the gift must be shared and used; otherwise it's as if the gift hadn't been given at all.

Prevenient grace is the grace that God has already offered to you. It's a gift under the tree with your name on it even before you know how to spell your name. Justifying grace is God's work in the person of Jesus Christ. Jesus' life, suffering, death, and resurrection help us unwrap God's gift and claim it as our own. Sanctifying Grace is the work of the Holy Spirit to transform who we are. It's the work of God that offers us freedom and power to use and share God's gift with our friends, enemies, and the whole of God's creation.

Sharing God's grace is easy when life is good and problems are few and far between. Drosselmeir presents Clara with a nutcracker as his final gift. Clara isn't quite sure what to think of it. The Nutcracker is dressed in beautiful military regalia, but its face is large and awkward with a strange gaping mouth. Clara's brother is jealous of her gift and tries to wrestle it away from her. He doesn't offer Clara a chance to share the gift. He wants it as his own, and *he wants it now*. Grace is offered, accepted, and shared—not deserved, taken, and held. When we approach grace as something we deserve—that we must take, protect, and defend—the gift is damaged. The Nutcracker's head snaps off, and Clara weeps, certain that her gift is forever ruined.

Holy Communion is an exercise in grace offered, received, and shared, which is why the way we celebrate Communion in my congregation is intentional and planned. I invite the congregation saying, "The table is set. All things are ready. When the Holy Spirit invites you to come, will you come?" This initially sent the ushers into a frenzy because no direction is given. You can run toward the front of the church, you can sit in prayer and wait until you are ready to receive, or you can remain seated in your pew and choose not to come forward at all (which is great for guests or persons from other traditions who would prefer to simply observe and not have attention brought to them). When people come forward, they are offered a piece of bread. It's already broken for them. After dipping the bread into the cup, they can kneel at the chancel rail for prayer, offer a gift to the food pantry, return to their seat, or whatever. It may seem chaotic, and perhaps it is, but it reminds me of another chaotic time that is filled with excitement and gifts: Christmas morning.

4. HEALER OF OUR EVERY ILL

After Drosselmeir heals the Nutcracker, he disappears from the heart of the story, as our focus shifts to Clara's fanciful dream of warring mice and soldiers. It might seem that Drosselmeir's role in the story is complete, he's served his purpose, and the story is moving on. Of course, Clara's godfather is not quite finished offering surprises and miracles, but where is he during all of the action? Sometimes it seems that God is rather distant at times, watching us at a from afar, waiting for opportune moments to intervene.

A church member once stopped me in the hallway following Sunday morning worship, massaging her temples through a grimaced face. "Reverend Rawle, I've been having migraines. The medicine isn't helping. Nothing is working. Can you pray for me?" At first I was selfishly delighted that her grimace was not related to the sermon, which had been my first guess, but I quickly noticed that she was really in need of some intervention. In seminary, we were taught that "Take up your mat and walk" (in reference to Jesus' healing of the paralyzed man at Capernaum[2]) is a dangerous prayer to utter. It is risky, and unashamedly bold, but I thought, "What the heck?" I held her face in my hands and I prayed, "May the Holy Spirit heal you of these debilitating migraines. In the name of the Father and of the Son and of the Holy Spirit." Almost immediately her face unfolded. One eye opened, and then the next. Her jaw, which had been clenched for longer than she could remember, slacked, and she said, "What did you do?"

Her pain was gone. We both parted ways knowing that something very special had happened.

Two weeks later I went to visit another member in the hospital. She had fallen and needed hip surgery. After spending a few minutes with her, I boldly and confidently prayed, "May the Holy Spirit strengthen you so that you will get out of bed and walk down the church aisle once again to your pew." Later that afternoon I received a phone call from the hospital that she had passed away. Healing can be complicated. If a migraine can vanish, why were there complications with a hip replacement? If Drosselmeir can mend a nutcracker, why does he disappear when Clara is threatened by the Mouse King? Sometimes it feels that God's presence is very near, and other times we shake our fist toward the heavens like the psalmists, saying, "Where are you, God?"

Jesus' healings in the Gospel are honest about this perplexity. He hears that Lazarus is near death, but instead of running to Bethany, Jesus waits two days. A lame man is carried by four friends and Jesus says to him, "Your sins are forgiven," to which the Pharisees reply, "Only God can forgive sin." Defiantly, Jesus answers, "Is it easier to say 'Your sins are forgiven,' or 'Take up your mat and walk?'" So the man took up his mat and walked away. A woman touches his cloak and Jesus says, "Your faith has made you well," and sometimes Jesus' healings seem to have nothing to do with the faith of the sick. Conceivably there are some who Jesus either couldn't or simply wouldn't heal. Maybe it's the case that healing is something more than the body can show.

During the Advent and Christmas season, we often talk about Jesus' birth as a healing light entering into a world of darkness, as in verse 4 of the hymn "The Lord is my Light," which reads:

> The Lord is my light, my all and in all;
> There is in his sight no darkness at all;
> He is my Redeemer, my Savior, and King;
> With saints and with angels his praises I sing.[3]

John 9 offers us a succession of stories of how this light not only shows us the way, but is the way itself. What does this healing light accomplish? First, Jesus' healing destroys false assumptions. It sheds light on the truth. At the beginning of John 9, the disciples ask whose sin caused a man's blindness, and Jesus replies, "No one's." Sometimes illness carries an undeserved stigma, the assumption that illness is a consequence of divine discontent or disfavor. Sometimes our mistakes create difficult consequences, but life is not nearly this predictable. Jesus spits on the ground, rubs the mud in the man's eyes, and tells him to wash in the pool of Siloam. When the man regains his sight, those who know him are confused. They ask him how he is now able to see, but the man isn't quite sure how to answer the question. They bring the man "who had formerly been blind" (John 9:13) to the Pharisees, which is when we discover that Jesus healed the man on the Sabbath.

Not only does Jesus' healing destroy our false assumptions, but it also restores dignity. Notice how the blind man's identity is beginning to change. In verse 13 the man is described as "the man who had formerly been blind." Later, in verse 18, he is "the man who had received his sight." Yes, Jesus healed his eyes, but he is also healing the eyes of those around the man. Interestingly, over the course of this story, the man who regains his sight begins to grow in his understanding of Christ, while the Pharisees become increasingly blind. In a way, this is the fulfillment of an Advent reading, Isaiah 40, which says that every valley will be lifted up and every mountain made low. Those who have been oppressed are being filled with a deep and abiding presence and understanding of Christ while the oppressors are becoming increasingly shallow and blind.

The third thing Jesus' healing accomplishes is dissolving fear. When the Pharisees aren't sure what to make of this man's healing, they interview his parents. They ask if they know how their son regained his sight. His parents force the story right back onto their son, knowing that anyone claiming Jesus is the Messiah will be put out of the synagogue. The Pharisees return to the man asking the same questions, but this time he questions *them* about their faith saying, "I have told you already, and you would not listen. Why do you want to hear it again? Do you also want to become his disciples?" (John 9:27). The man's eyes have been filled with truth, and when truth grabs a hold of you, fear has no place from which to hang.

Lastly, Jesus heals our faith. After the Pharisees exile the man from the synagogue Jesus finds him and says, "I came into this world for judgment so that those who do not see may see, and those who do see may become blind." So, what does healing look like? Drosselmeir mending a broken nutcracker is a physical healing that we can point to. It may seem that he becomes distant during Clara's dream, but what is it that brings the toy to life when Clara needs him? Could it be that Drosselmeir has been there all the time, but Clara could not see it? When the Nutcracker falls in his battle with the Mouse King, without warning or petition, Drosselmeir again appears, bringing him back to life. When Drosselmeir intervenes, it's easy to recognize his presence. When healing is tangible and physical it's easy to recognize and celebrate. It's the healing we can't see that relies on great faith. The light that Christ brings into the world destroys our false assumptions, restores our dignity and identity, dissolves our fear, and fills us with abundant life. Drosselmeir's absence points us to a profound truth about healing. When we are in need of healing, it's not that the Spirit puts our broken pieces back together; rather the Spirit fills the void, increasing our capacity to love. In other words, when Drosselmeir seems most absent is precisely when his work is most abundant.

5. AT THE END OF IT ALL

Drosselmeir enters the story unexpectedly, seemingly out of nowhere. He offers the children a prophetic puppet show with toys that appear to spring to life. He mends what is broken, and he gives life to what is thought to be dead. At the end of the story, Clara sees him amongst the crowd of revelers in a beautiful kingdom seemingly created just for her. The viewer realizes then that Drosselmeir is more than Clara's godfather in the story. Even though the story is told through Clara's eyes, the tale isn't exclusively hers. In other words, what we read and see on the stage is Clara's experience through the story Drosselmeir has created.

Recently a friend challenged me to share my ten favorite albums on social media. I accepted his challenge, but added a few of my own personal footnotes. My top ten excluded categories like hymns and soundtracks because those are lists in and of themselves. I also included albums that I have listened to in their entirety from start to finish in one sitting. This dramatically shrunk the list of possible albums to include because I rarely sit still long enough to even listen to one song from beginning to end.

As I was compiling my list, I noticed that many of the singles from my favorite albums were covers, songs that had been reinterpreted from another artist. For example, "What a Fool Believes," on Self's album *Gizmodgery* is outstanding (knowing that the album uses only children's toys as the instruments), but the song was originally performed by the Doobie Brothers. "Ring Them Bells" on the album *Follow Me Down* by Sarah Jarosz is a song that I listen to at least once a week, but it's originally a Bob Dylan creation. These songs were written for a particular audience for a particular reason, and I find it fascinating that when a song is reinterpreted for a different audience at a different time, the song can be just as fresh and meaningful as the original.

Maybe this is one of the reasons why I love preaching so much. Every Sunday I get to read ancient texts and offer them to a contemporary community. This can get tricky at times, especially when I offer a familiar story. When I was just starting out as an associate pastor, I always had the pulpit on the Sunday after Christmas and Easter for what I call "National Associate Pastor Sundays" (NAPS for short because napping is exactly what the congregation is doing the Sunday after Easter and Christmas). After preaching on the walk to Emmaus from Luke 24 for the fourth Sunday in a row after Resurrection Sunday, I found myself stuck.

What else am I supposed to say about this story? This prepared me well for Christmas Eve. The folks who enter the sanctuary on Christmas Eve are expecting to hear Luke's version of the Nativity, but dusting off your sermon from last year somehow misses the point. Sometimes just saying that Christ is born is enough, but not always. It's not that the congregation will remember what you've preached before, but an unoriginal message will feel uninspired, even if they can't put their finger on why.

I was stuck because I hadn't considered changing my perspective. I had been preaching as if I were a character in the story. So, one year I began thinking about whose voice was silent in the story. We've heard from shepherds, angels, and Mary, but what about Joseph? There was no room in the inn, but what might the Innkeeper be thinking about? Did God breathe a sigh of relief when Jesus took his first breath? Jesus is the Messiah, God's greatest gift to us. That doesn't change, but the way we get to this truth might look quite different from person to person.

The Nutcracker is Drosselmeir's story told through Clara's interpretation. Would the story change if we overheard it from another character's point of view? If we heard the story from the Nutcracker's perspective, would we view Drosselmeir differently? What might the Mouse King think of this great benefactor of the story? I think we can safely say whoever the main character is, Drosselmeir will still be seen and full of surprises, a great healer, and one who seems to lovingly stick around until the end.

This helps us understand whose story is really being told. If you can tell the Christmas story from the shepherds' points of view, Mary's perspective, and the angels' position, and still point to Jesus as the Messiah, then what we've discovered is that the proclamation is true. If Clara, the Nutcracker, and the Mouse King might all see Drosselmeir as a loving godfather (albeit for different reasons), then this is the truth on which the story hangs. In other words, we are called to proclaim God's story. Whether we use contemporary music or traditional hymns, sing "Silent Night" in English or German, or open presents Christmas Eve or Christmas morning, if Christ is proclaimed, then truth has been revealed.

Drosselmeir, as a godfather, like God the Father, is there in the beginning, middle, and ending of the story. Scripture talks about God as one who is, was, and is to come, and this is good news! A God who *is* means that we are not abandoned. A God who *was* means that we are forgiven. A God who *is to come* means that God can be trusted. One year, Christie and I had dueling 10:30 Friday morning Thanksgiving programs to attend. Mine started at the Broadmoor Day School, where I saw my daughter Annaleigh stand and not sing a word. Then I snuck out to head over to Eden Gardens Elementary School for an 11:00 gathering.

There are some things my daughter Isabelle doesn't care about, but the schedule is not one of them. If we say we are going to the park, she wants to know which park, what time we are leaving, and what time we are expecting to leave said park—and woe to the person who deviates from the agreed-upon schedule. So, the night before, I told her that I was not going to be in her classroom at 10:30, but that I would meet her on the playground at 11:00. She must have gotten mixed up, however, because when I got to the school, three teachers met me on the playground saying, "Isabelle will certainly be glad to see you." I saw her coming from a distance with tears rolling down her face. I gave her a big hug and said, "I told you I was going to be here." A God who is to come is a God whose promise can be trusted.

What are the promises? John writes, "To him who loves us and freed us from our sins by his blood, and made us to be a kingdom, priests serving his God" (Revelation 1:5-6). God loves us—present tense. This is the work of the God who is. God who freed us from our sins—past tense. This is the work of the God who was. A God who made us to be a kingdom—future. This is the work of the God who is to come. God loves us, has forgiven us, and has given us purpose for the future beginning today as servants to God and for each other. Through faith in Christ, our present, our past, and our future are held together in grace.

So now you know the ending of the story. I pray that knowing the ending doesn't spoil it for you; rather I pray it gives you hope. Before we know it, another year will pass and we will welcome another Advent. We will tell the story all over again, light the first candle of Advent, and sing "Come Thou Long-Expected Jesus." I pray we never tire of presently living a story that "was" about a promise, which will be. Salvation is a process, and let it begin today.

Devotion

GOD'S LOVE BECOMING REAL

For God so loved the world that he gave his only Son, so that everyone who believes in him may not perish but may have eternal life.

John 3:16

While they were there, the time came for her to deliver her child. And she gave birth to her firstborn son and wrapped him in bands of cloth, and laid him in a manger, because there was no place for them in the inn.

Luke 2:6-7

"In a hole in the ground there lived a hobbit."
"It was the best of times, it was the worst of times."
"A long time ago in a galaxy far, far away."
These words are famous opening lines from three well-known and treasured stories—*The Hobbit* by J. R. R. Tolkien, *A Tale of Two Cities* by Charles Dickens, and *Star Wars* by George Lucas. Whether it's in print or on the big screen, we love a good story; and Christmas is no exception. Stories such as *The Night Before Christmas* and *The Nutcracker* are beloved favorites that capture the childlike wonder of the season. Yet beyond its appeal and charm as a seasonal staple, *The Nutcracker* has rich symbolism that speaks to us of a much greater story.

Clara is cherished by her godfather, Drosselmeir, who gives her the gift of a toy nutcracker. The Nutcracker battles the evil Mouse King, only to be killed and then brought back to life by the godfather himself. The Nutcracker then brings Clara to his kingdom, where his subjects have anxiously awaited his return. It resonates with strong parallels to the gospel story—a story of God's love becoming real in our lives through the gift of Jesus Christ.

The original Christmas story begins in Luke 2 with a familiar Nativity scene involving a young couple, angels, shepherds, and the Christ child lying in a manger. But it is in John's Gospel where we find words that, in a sense, might serve as a famous first line for the story: "For God so loved the world that he gave his only Son…" (John 3:16). Though often associated with the end of Jesus' earthly life, this verse also speaks of the deep love that motivated God's gift of love made flesh on that first Christmas morning.

God's love becoming real in our lives is what the Christmas story is about. During Advent we wait for the One who reveals God's heart of love, a love so great that it gives *all* for us. This season as you prepare to celebrate the greatest story ever told, ask yourself this question: *How is God's love becoming real in my life?*

God of love, thank you for the gift of your love in Jesus— the greatest gift of all. Show me how I can fully unwrap this gift so that your love may become real in my life in new and exciting ways. Amen.

Chapter Three

THE MOUSE KING: CHANGING PERSPECTIVE

In the fifteenth year of the reign of Emperor Tiberius, when Pontius Pilate was governor of Judea, and Herod was ruler of Galilee, and his brother Philip ruler of the region of Ituraea and Trachonitis, and Lysanias ruler of Abilene, during the high priesthood of Annas and Caiaphas, the word of God came to John son of Zechariah in the wilderness.

Luke 3:1-2

The presents under the tree were never disappointing in my childhood home. Sure, I put on my list that I wanted a pony, but deep down inside I knew that wasn't going to happen. I was always excited to show my friends at school the cool toys I received. Well, with the exception of one. There was a kid who always seemed to have the best of the best. I remember one year I received a brand-new pair of Reebok Pumps for Christmas—you know, the shoes from the mid-1990s you could pump up with air so that you could slam dunk like Michael Jordan. I proudly wore them to school, knowing that my social capital would go through the roof. I was ready to reveal my prized possession to my classmate. I stood in horror when I saw him, not just with his own set of Pumps, but with the oh-so-exclusive Pumps design from the commercial that I had seen over and over again on television. His shoes were just that much better than mine.

This trend continued for many years. If I received a *Legend of Zelda* video game, he would have the limited-edition version. If I brought to school a TI-81 calculator after winter break, he would bring his TI-82. Even though we had spent several weeks singing about joy and love from the pews of the sanctuary, it was jealousy that consumed my thoughts. "Peace on earth, and mercy mild?" Not a chance!

Christmas can have a dark side. When John's Gospel tells us of Jesus' origin, we hear that Jesus is a light that shines in the darkness. Joseph must have been anxious when he discovered that Mary was pregnant because an angel has to tell him in a dream, "Do not be afraid to take Mary as your wife" (Matthew 1:20b). When Jesus is born, Herod becomes so fearful that he goes on a murderous rampage throughout Judea. The gospel is called "good news" because we are all too familiar with news being bad. Maybe there's a bit of the Mouse King in all of us, something within us that is more comfortable with the darkness than we care to admit.

1. LARGER THAN LIFE

While Clara sleeps under the Christmas tree, she notices a mouse not only slinking toward her, but towering over her. It is a frightening sight to see something large that is supposed to be small. Think of old 1950s monster movies like *Tarantula*, *Godzilla*, and *The Blob*. On the surface, a spider, lizard, and shapeless goo aren't scary at all because we normally are much larger in comparison. When the spider is suddenly bigger than we are, there seems to be little hope. Being small, weak, and outnumbered seems to be a primal fear deep within our being. Maybe this is why sometimes we feel helpless when looking at the sins of the world. Homelessness, poverty, and inequality seem almost "too big to fail." At first glance, these problems seem larger than any one person can handle. On the one hand, they are exactly that, because we are called together to be one body working together to build God's kingdom. We aren't called to do it alone. On the other hand, these problems might not be as large as we think.

Perspective matters. I am a huge fan of Walt Disney World. It's not about the rides or shows or delicious Dole Whips in Adventureland; rather what I find fascinating is how the Magic Kingdom in particular tells a story. They expertly use a technique called forced perspective so that guests literally see things in a certain way. This technique is used everywhere if you have eyes to see it (and I hope this doesn't spoil the experience for you). For example, when you enter into Main Street you might notice that the windows of the shops lining the streets are relatively low to the ground. This is so children can see into the stores and beg their parents for souvenirs, but it's also to make you feel safe.

When you look down Main Street toward the large Cinderella Castle in the center of the park, the park appears endless and larger than it really is. This gives you a sense of excitement for what lies ahead. The opposite is true when you are at the castle looking toward the exits. From this point of view, the exits seem relatively close, which fills every stroller-pushing parent with hope and relief. On a smaller scale, when you go on an attraction like the Haunted Mansion or Peter Pan's flight, your ride vehicle moves and turns to show you specific scenes of the story Disney has created. The ride forces you to look at certain things at certain times. Of course, you can look the other way, but in doing so you will see extension cords, exit signs, and backstage areas. This destroys the illusion.

Forced perspective is neither good nor bad in and of itself. If we are being honest, the church uses a kind of forced perspective every time we gather for worship. Whether it's stained glass windows or screens, a choir or a band, a pastor in a robe or sneakers and spiky hair, or the order of worship, all of these create a specific environment through which we tell God's story. What we sometimes don't realize is how powerful this can be. When the message and the environment are in contrast, it's difficult for the message to be heard. It's like preaching about the importance of hospitality when there aren't any greeters welcoming guests or singing "Simple Gifts" while raising a golden chalice. When our message is confused, sin sees an advantage. Sin forces our perspective in thinking that poverty is too big, homelessness is too pervasive, and problems are solved through legislation, petitions, or words in a Discipline.

From Main Street, Cinderella Castle looks like it's hundreds of feet tall and built with stone, gold, and limestone. Actually, it's 189 feet tall (less than half the height of the Washington Monument) and made with scaffolding, plaster, and paint. In order to see things as they really are, sometimes it means getting very close. In other words, we cannot end poverty without being in ministry with the poor.

This is also why God put on flesh and was born in a lowly manger. In a way, Jesus is "God up close." Through Christ, God changes our perspective on what it means to be powerful or blessed or righteous. As we move closer to Christmas, God's story begins to strip away palaces, borders, and earthly power. God's story began with humanity and the divine walking with one another in a garden. Then God led the ancient Israelites through a pillar of cloud by day and a pillar of fire by night. God was in the tabernacle wandering with the chosen people. Then, the Israelites wanted a king like the other nations had. The space between God and humanity was filled with walls, rulers, and an economy that valued some over others.

When leaning into Advent, you get the sense that the space between God and humanity grows increasingly smaller. We trade soldiers for shepherds, Jerusalem for Bethlehem, and rulers for rural peasants. It's like God is trying desperately to walk in the garden with us, and the only way to do it is to topple the walls, tear down the borders, and trade a crown of gold for a crown of thorns.

In keeping with the topic of perspective, when the space between us and God is small, the problems of the world don't seem nearly as large. Several years ago, a group of divinity students wanted to tackle homelessness in their city. At first it seemed impossible, but through prayer and discernment and asking lots of questions with the homeless, they devised a plan that is painfully simple. They took the number of homeless families and the number of area churches and discovered that if each area church footed the bill for 2.4 families a year, there would be no one left homeless in the city. One church discovered that housing two families a year was roughly the amount they were spending on colored paper in the copy room. Of course, there were other details to consider such as location and affordability, but asking churches to consider doing Christ's work without colored paper in the office is a lot less daunting than asking, "Will you help end homelessness?"

When we look at the world from a distance, things aren't always what they seem. What seems to be a looming fortress might just be plaster and paint. God's movement toward us in Jesus is divine permission to move closer to one another, especially those who have been left out of our Main Streets and our castles. But what happens when we move in close and the problems are larger than we are? It could be that Clara is imagining mice larger than herself, but it seems real enough. When there seems to be little hope is precisely when the Nutcracker wakes up!

2. BATTLES PERCEIVED AND REAL

The bugle has sounded, and the skirmish begins. The Nutcracker's army and the Mouse King's henchmen are locked into a back-and-forth battle. It's not quite clear what they are fighting about. Does the Mouse King perceive Clara as a threat? Is he so evil that any hint of innocence has to be vanquished? Could it be that fighting is simply a way to pass the time? Knowing what you are fighting for is important, but even a vague purpose doesn't make the battle any less real.

Sometimes Christmas can seem like a back-and-forth battle. Planning a Christmas gathering is simple enough when the guest list is expected and routine. Growing up, I knew our Christmas rhythm, and I could easily anticipate who would be around the tree come Christmas lunch. My sisters and I would wake up our parents early in the morning to see what Santa had left near the chimney. My grandparents would eventually arrive in the living room with coffee in hand. Around lunchtime, my uncle and aunt would arrive with new presents for our second round of gift-giving.

We would gather for a late Christmas lunch, and we eventually went our separate ways either to play with our toys or to take a much-needed nap.

All of this changed when I got married. The blessing in changing my routine was that there were more people in my life with whom I could share Christmas…but nowhere in the Bible does it say that blessings are easy to swallow. Whose parents' house will be the "Christmas house"? Should we try to see everyone on Christmas morning, or alternate years, or should we just do our own thing and see family later in the week? I'm sure many of you can relate. Eventually I became a pastor, which made things more complicated. With family living in different corners of the state and a midnight Christmas Eve sermon to offer, gathering together on Christmas Day became very difficult.

Then my wife and I became parents, which added an additional column (or two) to the Christmas gathering spreadsheet. It's not easy to see your children open presents on Christmas morning and then tell them to leave the gifts behind to get in the car to visit family for a few days. And we aren't the only ones in our family who are married with kids.

It's complicated. It isn't easy. Sometimes it feels like a back-and-forth battle between phone calls, texts, and calendars, but at least we know why it takes so long to make a plan. The good news is we love being together, and even when the planning of our gatherings becomes a royal pain, we know it's all worth it. The intentions are always good.

It's like the unfortunate debate I often hear of people wondering if it's okay to say "Merry Christmas" to someone. Of course it is. It's also okay to say "Happy Holidays" and to say "thank you" when someone says it back. It's not nearly as important to say "Merry Christmas" as it is to create an environment in which those who believe and those who do not are welcome. In other words, sometimes we confuse evangelism with apologetics, the discipline of defending one's faith. Sharing the Christian story and inviting people to become a part of it will always be more important than defending it. At the very least, Jesus seemed to only defend the faith against the religious elite who thought they had God all figured out.

When we complain about Starbucks cups, "Christmas break" being changed to "winter break," or department stores taking "Christmas" off the sales-rack advertisements, our apologetics gets the best of us. Maybe the anger we feel is from regret that we've forgotten how to share the Christmas message without coffee, the government, or retail spaces. Our discipleship becomes defense without invitation, which means we build walls that end up protecting nothing.

3. People, Look East

Out of nowhere a mouse, larger and uglier than the others, appears. Clara realizes that this crowned mouse looks just like the one in the puppet show. Could it be that the puppet show has come to life? Will the puppet show's happy ending be the ending she will experience? When you're surrounded by mice twice your size, there's little time to ponder. The Nutcracker springs into action, but it doesn't take long before he and Clara realize they are outnumbered. Suddenly a bugle sounds from the Christmas tree, and several toy soldiers come to their aid.

One thing I love about the Christmas story is that it is not something you can keep to yourself. It calls people together. The angels tell the shepherds to go and see the child. Wise men from the east "traverse afar" to see the child king. When Jesus first meets the disciples, they ask him where he is staying. Instead of giving them an address, he says, "Come and see" (John 1:39). When we decorate our living room tree, we always decorate it with "come and see" in mind. As I mentioned before about our tree, every ornament tells a story. Some ornaments are "Baby's first Christmas" pictures, others remind us of our trip to England. Others we've collected while visiting national parks, and others simply reflect the things we love. Every year we invite the church staff over to our home for Christmas dinner, and we can't wait to show them the new additions of our Christmas tree story.

The Christmas story is evangelistic. It is meant to be shared. "O come, let *us* adore him," the hymn invites us to sing together. Advent hymns are few and far between, and the ones we do find in the hymnal aren't usually topping the Billboard charts. Often when thinking about Advent, we talk about the season as a time of personal preparation. It certainly is that, but sometimes we miss that preparing for Christ is something that you cannot do alone. One of my favorite hymns beautifully and joyfully emphasizes Advent as a time of evangelistic preparation. "People, Look East," written by Eleanor Farjeon in 1928, points us to the importance of communal hospitality as we await Christ's birth.

> People, look east and sing today:
> Love, the Guest, is on the way.[1]

How might our Christmas celebrations change if we decorated the tree, hung the lights, and wrapped gifts as if love might be a guest in our home? Who in our congregations are most in need of love to make a visit? Inviting love into our lives makes us vulnerable, and vulnerability lies at the heart of the Christmas story. God entered the world as a baby, born to young first-time parents. I remember leaving the hospital with our firstborn child, and I have never been more scared in my life. I could not believe that they were letting us leave the hospital with the small human being in our care. My mind was flooded with a hundred things that could have gone wrong. What if she doesn't nurse well? What happens if she doesn't fall asleep after we rock her? When she does fall asleep, how can we be sure that she's breathing? I'm a relatively responsible grown-up, but I have never been so unsure of my ability to be a contributing member of society. You can read every parenting book on the planet, but none of the advice seems to matter until you cradle your child in your arms in your home your first night away from the hospital. What was God thinking being born as a child?

We invited this new child into our home, and all of our insecurities were unmasked. What we discovered is that the child was not nearly as vulnerable as we were. When you invite someone into your life, it's difficult to hide your imperfections. But that's the point. A colleague of mine recently called hoping I could offer wisdom on how to balance writing with being a pastor, a father, a husband, and all of the many hats we all wear. I didn't have much advice to offer other than to say I struggle with the same things. We had a long talk about how clergy tend to think that being a leader means having no faults. Will our congregation trust us if we move forward with a bad idea? What might happen if my sermon bombs? What if we take a risk on a new ministry, and it fails?

It's like the first prayer I offered as a ministry intern. I had the good fortune to have a student intern position at Myers Park United Methodist Church in Charlotte, NC, my first summer in seminary. Rev. Dr. James C. Howell allowed me to give the offering prayer on my first Sunday. I was nervous, but I was ready. I had prepared an eloquent prayer, committed it to memory, and waited to impress the congregation with my excellent verbosity. The ushers brought forward the offering plates. I turned to face the altar/table, lifted the plates high with veneration, bowed my head, and started to pray. Halfway through my prayer, my arms started to shake. The offering plates were heavier than I had anticipated, and to say that I work out would be a lie. I started concentrating on not dropping the plates, which means I had stopped concentrating on my words. The last line of my prayer was supposed to be, "...and let us continue to lift up the city, Charlotte," only I didn't say "city." You try saying "city Charlotte" over and over again and see what happens....And as you can imagine, I was mortified! A woman approached me after worship, shook my hand, and said, "Thank you." "For what?" I replied. She answered, "For being human."

4. IN THE DAYS OF KING HEROD

I'm not sure of the Mouse King's royal lineage, but having a king as the villain of the story is certainly poignant when thinking about Jesus' birth. After a brief preface explaining to whom Luke's Gospel is written, Luke begins his story with "In the days of King Herod." It seems that history is a story of kings and queens, which means it's a miracle we know anything at all about Jesus. Luke offers an interesting and subtle message about the rulers of Jesus' day and what little power they really had in God's kingdom.

Power and influence rarely come from a title or position. Several years ago, a congregation in North Carolina invited a new clergyperson to lead the congregation. The church members called her "Reverend," welcomed her to offer the sermon each Sunday, and followed her lead in committee meetings and mission projects...until there was a disagreement between the pastor and the church administrator about the use of the prayer room in the fellowship hall. The pastor wanted the room to remain open as often as possible so that folks would have a place to spend time in prayer. The church administrator wanted the room locked as often as possible because the room's furnishings might be susceptible to theft. Having a prayer room too elegantly decorated to be used for prayer is an altogether different conversation, but this debate revealed the true shepherd of the worshiping community. It wasn't long before the prayer room was perpetually locked outside of the Sunday school hour on Sunday mornings. After all, the church administrator's name was literally on the outside of the fellowship hall if there was any question who was really in charge. For the record, if your prayer room is too nice to be used, you're doing it wrong.

Luke offers a similar, yet more subtle, commentary on where power rests in the Gospel story. "In the days of King Herod," may begin the story, but nothing more about Herod is mentioned until after Jesus' ministry begins. In Luke 3 Herod returns, but *how* he returns is precisely Luke's point:

> *In the fifteenth year of the reign of Emperor Tiberius, when Pontius Pilate was governor of Judea, and Herod was ruler of Galilee, and his brother Philip ruler of the region of Ituraea and Trachonitis, and Lysanias ruler of Abilene, during the high priesthood of Annas and Caiaphas, the word of God came to John son of Zechariah in the wilderness.*
>
> *Luke 3:1-2*

Did you catch that? Luke sounds like a butler announcing entering guests to a political dinner party, but concludes his proclamation with "the word of God came to John." Here are very important people doing seemingly important things, but the word of God came to John. It's subtle, but scandalously important. It's like detailing the niceties of a prayer room, but ending your list with "And the Holy Spirit was with the woman locked outside." Again, please don't lock your prayer room.

The Gospel of Matthew suggests King Herod knew how little power and influence he had. When the wise men visit Herod in the palace asking, "Where is the child who has been born King of the Jews?" (Matthew 2:2), this fills Herod with terror and dread for several reasons. First, these men from the east have announced that this child is the born ruler of Jews, not appointed by Caesar. From where did this child receive such authority? This child signals not only the end of Herod's rule, but also an end to Herod's dynasty. Secondly, these men are not Jews. They are from a land Caesar doesn't rule. If they know about this child, who else might be coming to pay him homage? In other words, not only will this child supplant Herod as ruler, but this king might even be greater. It's one thing to lose power. It's another thing to be completely eclipsed.

Herod asks the men to reveal the child's location because he too wants to pay him homage. Although Matthew doesn't specify this, we can assume that Herod's desire to praise Jesus is less than genuine. When Herod discovers that the wise men have failed to honor his request, he spirals into a rampage ordering the slaughter of all male children under the age of two years old. Then Herod disappears from the story altogether (his son, also named Herod, assumes the throne). The king is remembered for his fear, anxiety, and murderous ways. Herod enters the story with little fanfare, and he exists with even less.

The Mouse King is a bit of a mystery as well. He appears out of nowhere, bent on harming Clara for unspoken reasons. He doesn't seem to have a vendetta or political cause. He just wants to cause harm. This is why, in Clara's dream, the Mouse King represents her brother, Fritz. Family is a funny thing. Early in ministry I referred to the congregation as our "church family," because when I was growing up family represented safety, joy, and a whole lot of fun. I realized far too late that the word "family" isn't always so well-received. Now that I'm a parent, our family is still a lot of fun, but not always. My wife and I celebrate when our kids get out of school for their winter break. The mornings are not nearly as hectic, afternoon rehearsals and activities are canceled until later in January, and we have a lot of time simply to be together. But sometimes in itself that can be a frustration.

A few days after the semester break begins, we find ourselves peeking at the calendar to see when classes resume. The squabbles are simple and mostly innocent—"Dad, she's wearing my favorite socks," "Mom, he won't give me the remote control, and his turn is over," and so on. However, over several weeks, the simple and innocent become constant and annoying. My favorite squabble from my own childhood (can you have a favorite squabble?) occurred when my family was taking a vacation. My sisters were sitting next to each other in the back seat, which was an unavoidable recipe for disaster. Throughout the trip they were going back and forth, trading glances and threatening to cross the imaginary line that separated them. My younger sister, who interestingly enough is a lawyer today, would put her face right next to my other sister's face, not officially touching her, although the molecules separating them were few and far between. My other sister got so frustrated she yelled out, "Mom! She's breathing *my* air!" When you can no longer share air with each other, it's time to stop the car and take a break. I imagine that when they fell asleep later that afternoon while on the road, they were dreaming about each other as Mouse Queens.

The Mouse King in Clara's dream is menacing, threatening, and dangerous. Could it be that this villain is simply her overblown reaction to her pesky little brother? Is there something deeper and more perilous at work? Herod certainly thought that a child born King of the Jews was a heralding of the end of everything Herod knew. Maybe Herod's fear was real, knowing that a child born, and not appointed, to be king would certainly unmask his illegitimacy as ruler. The problem is Herod was unaware that Jesus wasn't after an earthly throne. It's true that Jesus announces a kingdom where the mountains will be razed and the rich are sent away empty, but it is a kingdom in which no one is beyond redemption and forgiveness. There is mercy offered to all of us, even those who lock their prayer rooms. Please don't lock your prayer room.

5. THE DEATH OF THE MOUSE KING

The Nutcracker and his soldiers eventually vanquish the terrifying and treacherous Mouse King and his henchmen. Clara is saved, and the story continues, but there's a cost. When the Mouse King falls at the hand of the Nutcracker's sword, the Nutcracker also dies. Christ's birth is certainly good news, as the angel announces, but sometimes good doesn't feel all that good.

One of my friends recently graduated from a ninety-day rehabilitation facility for substance abuse. I couldn't be more proud of him. First, to have the maturity to check himself into a facility, recognizing that his life wasn't where it needed to be, is a tremendous step, and arguably the most difficult. He called me not long ago to let me know that he had returned home. We had the most mature conversation I think we've ever had. I spent a great deal of time congratulating him, and talking about how happy I was that he was returning home. I must have sounded too excited about his accomplishment, or at the very least, I must have communicated that the work he had invested in changing his life was over. He sympathetically reminded me that the difficult work was just beginning.

If you've ever been addicted to something, or know someone who has, you know that the addiction never really goes away. It's one thing to stay sober in a facility under supervision. It's another thing to remain sober when you return home. When my friend mentioned that the real struggle was just beginning, staying sober is what I thought he meant. He again gracefully corrected me saying, "No, the difficult thing will now be seeking forgiveness from my friends and family." His response was both humbling and amazing.

Christ's birth is good news. Salvation is here. The kingdom of God is at hand. God's grace in the person of Jesus Christ is freely offered to all, but saying that grace is freely received isn't entirely true. There's a footnote that must be mentioned. Footnotes are important, and without them we might make frustrating mistakes. One afternoon while teaching a preaching class for the Shreveport District Lay Servant School, I received a phone call from my wife that she had a flat tire. I ended the class early and rushed out to change the tire. Although I am terrible at fixing or repairing anything, this task I can handle. In fact, when changing a tire, I'm very much like the dad in *A Christmas Story*. Changing a tire is like a challenge against myself. Would I break a personal record this time?

I found our minivan on the side of the road, and quickly got to work. I grabbed the tools from under the floorboard, started loosening the lug nuts, and jacked up the car quickly. I was convinced this would be a personal best. I quickly removed four of the lug nuts, but then there was one with a design I had never seen. I attacked it with the tire iron, pushing and twisting to the point where I almost passed out. It wasn't moving at all. I looked at the lug nut with greater intention and noticed that it was perfectly round with a star shape in the middle. After this discovery, I knew that my hexagonal tire iron was no longer any use to me. I swallowed my pride and opened the manual to see if it offered any help. Step number six read, "Remove lug nuts." That's it. That's all. Remove lug nuts? That's what I'm trying to do! There was no footnote. There was no asterisk sending me to search for more information. "Remove lug nuts" was all that was offered.

I took fast hold of the touchstone keychain in my pocket so that I didn't say something in front of the kids that I would later regret, like Ralphie in *A Christmas Story*. I texted a few friends and posted a picture on Facebook asking for advice. Come to find out that this different lug nut was a special theft deterrent feature that I was not fortunate enough to know that I had paid for. There was a special key in the glove box that you attach to the tire iron in order to remove this particular lug nut. Once I figured this out, almost two hours after leaving my preaching class, changing the tire was easy. My tire-changing time was now ruined, and all of this could have been prevented by a single footnote saying something to the effect of "Check glove box for key."

Footnotes are important. They can sometimes change the entire context of what you're reading.[*] Take John 8:1-11, for example, which contains a footnote suggesting that this story probably isn't original to John's Gospel. Or try looking up Acts 8:37, which in many newer Bibles exists only as a footnote. There

---

[*] But not in this case. Just seeing if you would check.

needs to be a great footnote to the old hymn "Freely, Freely" (*The United Methodist Hymnal*, 389), which reads, "God forgave my sin in Jesus' name, I've been born again in Jesus' name." The footnote should say, "If you are born again, something had to die."

For my friend who returned home from rehab, his love for alcohol had to die in order to begin seeking forgiveness and reconciliation. Paul announces in Romans 10:15, "How beautiful are the feet of those who bring good news." The announcement of Good News is certainly joyful, but be sure to check the footnote. Paul is quoting Isaiah 52:7, one of the many verses we like to read during Advent—"How beautiful upon the mountains are the feet of the messenger who announces peace, who brings good news, who announces salvation...." This messenger is one who will prosper and astonish many. He shall startle the nations, and kings will shut their mouths in his presence. This messenger, as Isaiah goes on to say,

> *...has borne our infirmities*
> *and carried our diseases;*
> *yet we accounted him stricken,*
> *struck down by God, and afflicted.*
> *But he was wounded for our transgressions,*
> *crushed for our iniquities...*
> *For he was cut off from the land of the living.*
> *Isaiah 53:4-5a, 8b*

This Christ-child, who came to announce God's good news for the world, is also the one who died and rose again so that we might find abundant life and resurrection. Grace is freely offered, but receiving this grace, walking with it, sharing it with one another and the world means that our love for the things that distract us from God's love must be crucified with Christ. Maybe this is why the angel announcing good news calls for the shepherds to have no fear? It's fearful to let go of the things sedating us to the needs of our brothers and sisters. Whether it's our own affluence or selfishness, addiction to a substance, or greed, accepting this grace is a costly discipleship. Maybe there's a Mouse King in all of us that needs to be slain in order for our feet to match the beauty of Christ's?

Devotion

THE COST OF CHRISTMAS

In that region there were shepherds living in the fields, keeping watch over their flock by night. Then an angel of the Lord stood before them, and the glory of the Lord shone around them, and they were terrified. But the angel said to them, "Do not be afraid; for see—I am bringing you good news of great joy for all the people: to you is born this day in the city of David a Savior, who is the Messiah, the Lord.

Luke 2:8-11

The song says, "It's the most wonderful time of the year," but if we're honest, sometimes Christmas is a struggle. Just as the Nutcracker and his soldiers fight the evil Mouse King and his horde on Christmas Eve, so we have our own battles to face—things that just don't go away and give us a break when the holidays roll around. In fact, for some of us Christmas can be one of the most difficult times of the year, intensifying feelings of loneliness, anxiety, depression, and fear.

Though the Nutcracker and his soldiers defeat the Mouse King, saving Clara, there still is a cost: the Nutcracker dies along with the Mouse King. Eventually the Nutcracker is restored and brought to life again, but for a time all seems lost. It can be the same in our own lives. We know the good news of the Christmas story, yet sometimes good just doesn't feel so good. Even the shepherds who were receiving the most wondrous news in all of history were uncertain and afraid and had to be comforted and encouraged to focus on the joy of the message: *a Savior, the Messiah, has come!*

The story of the shepherds reminds us that regardless of how we may be feeling or what we may be facing, there is hope for tomorrow. The Christ-child who came to announce God's good news for the world is the same one who, after counting the cost, died and rose again so that we might have abundant life now and for all eternity. The hope of this resurrection life is the good news that banishes all fear.

This Advent may we not only receive the gift of God's grace freely offered to us but also generously share it with others—with all who are burdened and in need of peace, hope, and joy. And as we do, may we trade our fear for the joy of the one who promises to be with us always.

God of grace, thank you for the good news that is ours in Jesus Christ—that because of his sacrifice, we have the promise of abundant life here and now and the hope of eternal life to come. May this good news be like a brilliant light shining in the darkness, dispelling any anxiety, fear, or sadness that would threaten to rob me of your joy. Amen.

Chapter Four

THE NUTCRACKER: THE GREATEST GIFT

I am bringing you good news of great joy for all the people.

Luke 2:10

Have you ever wondered why people put trees in their living rooms to celebrate Jesus' birth? It's rather peculiar when you think about it. Socks by the fireplace? That's a fire hazard! Why does Santa enjoy cookies and milk? I remember after my father had a heart attack, we started leaving carrot sticks, apples, and a tall glass of water by the fireplace for Santa to munch on. What a curious change to such a long-standing tradition.

The Nutcracker story itself contains Christmas pictures and images that both shaped and were shaped by our traditions. "The Nutcracker and the Mouse King," a German short story written in 1816 by E. T. A. Hoffmann, inspired the ballet. And because many of our American Christmas traditions were shaped by German culture, the Christmas celebration at the beginning of the story looks familiar to us. There's a Christmas tree surrounded by presents, a family has gathered together for a meal, the weather outside is frightful, and a nutcracker is given as a special present. Have you considered what *The Nutcracker* story might be like if it had been written in South Africa? How would the story change if E. T. A. Hoffmann had been Korean? Maybe there would be no nutcracker at all in the story if it took place in Chile.

The angel in Luke's Gospel says, "I am bringing you good news of great joy for all the people." If "all" truly means all, then this good news will be shared in different languages, through different traditions, with different music, food, and celebrations. The nutcracker Drosselmeir offers to Clara represents God's greatest gift to us in the person of Jesus Christ. This gift points us beyond our beautiful and unique cultural celebrations, to our commonality wrapped up together in swaddling clothes lying in a manger. This gift from God is a joy and salvation that knows no border, boundary, flag, or anthem. What we discover at the end of this story is that "all" just might mean *all*.

1. THE GIFT WE WANT OR NEED

For Clara, the nutcracker is a precious gift, though at first she's confused as to why it is so special. Why would she need a nutcracker, anyway? She wasn't expecting to get into a wrestling match with her brother, or to have to fight off the Mouse King.

Maybe she would have been better off if the toy hadn't been given at all. Have you ever been in a situation when you've received exactly what you wanted, but getting what you wanted led to receiving lots of things you didn't? When I was in college, I asked my parents for a dog for Christmas. Since I was so close to graduation, I felt that I was responsible enough for the challenge of a puppy in my apartment. My parents surprised me with a Dachshund that I named Boudreaux (I had two Dachshunds when I was a child, so I've always had a soft spot for this interesting breed). At first it was exciting to show Boudreaux off to my friends, take him on walks, and play fetch with him outside.

Then he started chewing everything in sight, howling all night, and ruining my roommates' things. It was becoming clear that it was either me or the dog who was going to have to leave. My parents and I eventually found Boudreaux a new home with friends of the family. I did take a little pleasure in knowing that the first Christmas after we gave him away, Boudreaux opened the family's Christmas presents all by himself one night. Maybe his behavior wasn't totally my fault.

Sometimes the things we want aren't the things we need, and the things we need aren't what we want. Clara didn't ask for the nutcracker, and she wasn't quite sure that she wanted it. Recently someone asked me why during worship we say a Prayer of Confession, a public and communal prayer asking for God's forgiveness, on Sunday mornings. We often use the following, which is found in *The United Methodist Hymnal*:

> Merciful God,
> we confess that we have not loved you with our
> whole heart.
> We have failed to be an obedient church.

We have not done your will,
we have broken your law,
we have rebelled against your love,
we have not loved our neighbors,
and we have not heard the cry of the needy.
Forgive us, we pray.
Free us for joyful obedience,
through Jesus Christ our Lord.
Amen.[1]

"Shouldn't that just be between me and God?" this person asked. Well, yes, but confession is also between neighbor and neighbor. Some might see a public prayer of confession as a reminder of how we fall short of God's glory. And it definitely is, but I've learned that most of us are well aware of the place we fall short. There's a difference between knowing our sin and having the courage to seek forgiveness for our shortcomings. More to the point, confession is a reminder that we are in need of God's grace. This prayer is incomplete without hearing its pardon:

Hear the good news:
Christ died for us while we were yet sinners;
that proves God's love toward us.
In the name of Jesus Christ, you are forgiven![2]

The nutcracker was a gift Clara didn't ask for and didn't think she needed. Jesus is certainly the gift we need from God, but is Jesus the gift we want from God? On the one hand, of course. It's like the African-American spiritual, "Give Me Jesus": "Give me Jesus, give me Jesus, you may have all this world, but give me Jesus." Jesus was a healer and a servant. He opened the eyes of the blind and made the lame walk. He fed and taught thousands. This is a beautiful and most certainly wanted gift from God. In John's Gospel, Jesus is the Bread of Life, the Living Water, and the Good Shepherd. When the baby Jesus is presented in the Temple for dedication, Simeon gives praise to God saying, "Master, now you are dismissing your servant in peace, according to your word; for my eyes have seen your salvation" (Luke 2:29-30). Jesus fulfills our desire for peace, spiritual nourishment, and the way that leads to life.

But on the other hand, Jesus also asks something of us. Jesus calls us to love our enemies, turn the other cheek, give to the poor, ask for nothing in return, and carry the cross in obedience. Sometimes Jesus doesn't seem to be the gift we want. Often we want to feel comfortable, successful, affluent, and proud. Sharing the gospel can make us quite uncomfortable when we are in ministry with those who don't think, look, or act like we do. It's not that we shouldn't strive to be successful, but Christ's success in the world is often difficult to put on a spreadsheet or measure by metrics. Jesus was pretty clear about how we should use our wealth in the world, and it's not about building larger storehouses to hoard our abundance. We can certainly celebrate with one another, but our boasting should always be pointed toward the work that Christ has done. We do not reach out in concern and service to the world because we need to earn our salvation or divine favor; rather the work that we offer is the fruit of the grace we've received. Following Christ isn't so much about being reminded of sin as much as it is about being reminded of the grace we've received, and how we should share that grace with the world. At times, Jesus might not seem like the gift we want, but Christ certainly is the gift we need.

The nutcracker is the gift Clara needs. When she finds herself surrounded by the Mouse King and his henchmen, the Nutcracker springs into action. When the dust settles at the end of the fight, we discover that the Nutcracker is wounded, and he falls motionless on the floor. In her disbelief, she hears the footsteps of her godfather, who offers her comfort and brings the Nutcracker back to life... but this time the Nutcracker is different. When he opens his eyes, he's "more real" than before. He's no longer made of wood. He's now flesh and blood. When the Nutcracker comes back to life, he takes Clara on a journey to a kingdom filled with people from all corners of the world celebrating their arrival.

2. CALL AND RESPONSE

"Being perplexed" varies in meaning. I am constantly plagued in my ministry by soundboard issues. Granted, I'm a bit of a snob when it comes to worship music and sanctuary sound balance, so I do a fair amount of tinkering with the soundboard, to the chagrin of many a volunteer. We have a fantastic volunteer behind the board in the church I currently serve, but the audio production during worship has had some peculiar results. Both he and I find ourselves often scratching our heads as we search for the cause of the problem. One Sunday morning, there was an echo delay, but it was only happening in a few, seemingly unrelated channels. The bass guitar would sound twice when played, as would choir microphone number four. I was absolutely perplexed because I could not understand why the problem was happening. Come to find out there was a bug in our digital soundboard that would select at random certain channels and change the production settings. Having an echo delay is a great thing, if you are Edge (U2's lead guitarist), but happening at random with some of the choir mics is a maddening conundrum.

Sometimes we are perplexed because we don't understand. Why is someone acting that way? Why did my check engine light come on? Why did I think that the "terrible twos" ended when children turned three? But this isn't the only definition of "perplexed." Every morning it was a struggle to get my oldest daughter to wear her mandatory kindergarten uniform. Getting her to wear this fleece pullover was a daily negotiation between her refusals and my frustration. One morning I took a deep breath and asked her to put on her fleece, and she quickly and pleasantly replied, "Sure, daddy," without a fight. I immediately knew something wasn't right. I was perplexed, not because I didn't understand what was going on, but because I didn't believe what I was hearing. Perplexity isn't always rooted in ignorance. Sometimes we are perplexed at the unexpected.

My daughter grabbed her fleece out of her backpack, but the fleece was dripping wet. This sweet, innocent child looked up at me and said, "Oh no, daddy. It's wet. I guess I can't wear it." The amount of premeditation needed to pull off a stunt of this magnitude is rather frightening. Seeing her craftiness is like looking into a mirror, which is why I countered her masterful plan by pulling out the spare fleece from the laundry room saying, "You've got to do better than that!"

When the angel Gabriel announces to Mary that she is going to give birth, we hear that she is "much perplexed by his words and ponder[s] what sort of greeting this might be" (Luke 1:29). Mary asks the angel, "How can this be, since I am a virgin?" Her confusion at this unexpected announcement is perfectly legitimate. We should admire Mary's courage in prodding the angel for more information. In fact, this call and response places Mary squarely in the tradition of the great prophets from the Hebrew Scriptures. When God says, "Moses, free my people," Moses replies, "What will I say to them? How will they believe me?" Or when God says to Isaiah, "Offer my word to my people," Isaiah responds with, "God, I am a man of unclean lips." And when God says to Jeremiah, "I appointed you before you were born," Jeremiah answers, "Lord, I am too young, and I don't know how to speak."

This prophetic call and response is part of a pattern we see over and over again when God calls his people into doing God's work: divine confrontation (the angel appears), introductory word (Greetings, favored one), commission (you will bear a son), objection (how can this be), reassurance (the Holy Spirit will come upon you), and sign (Elizabeth is also with child).

Two things distinguish this holy interaction with the other prophetic patterns we have witnessed. First, Gabriel's commission and reassurance propels Mary into a hopeful future with an intensity the other prophets hadn't heard. Notice how many times the angel uses the future tense:

> You **will** conceive in your womb and bear a son, and you **will** name him Jesus. He **will** be great, and **will** be called the Son of the Most High, and the Lord God **will** give to him the throne of his ancestor David. He **will** reign over the house of Jacob forever, and of his kingdom there **will** be no end....
>
> "The Holy Spirit **will** come upon you, and the power of the Most High **will** overshadow you; therefore the child to be born **will** be holy; he **will** be called Son of God."
>
> Luke 1:31-33, 35

Second, and maybe more astonishing than this definitive proclamation, is Mary's abundant and steadfast faith in accepting what God is asking her to do. It's almost as if Mary interrupts the angel's goodbye like the woman who held fast to Jesus' cloak, interrupting his journey to heal Jairus's daughter. Before the angel departs she says, "Let it be with me according to your word." For the first time in Scripture, there is a prophetic response of affirmation. It seems that none of the other prophets were as bold.

Mary allows herself to be overshadowed by the Holy Spirit. Sometimes I fear that it is Christmas rather than Christ that overshadows us this time of year. It's not enough to keep Christ *in* Christmas. Christ *is* Christmas. It is scandalous to announce God's intervention in the world through peace, hope, love, and joy, and then to celebrate the birth of a baby. With choirs shouting "Joy to the World," Christmas trees towering over the altar cross, and the hustle and bustle of retail registers, you might expect that Christmas Eve would herald a mighty warrior or stoic king. But God offers us a baby, a dependent child who is placed in a manger because there is no room in the inn. When Christ is born, we are overshadowed by a humility and great love that embarrasses the baubles to which we've surrendered our time to wrap, ship, and exchange.

We should be perplexed over God's prodigal hope in such a counter expression of power and majesty. As you may have noticed, I love singing "Silent Night" at the end of our Christmas Eve service. In this moment, we allow the Holy Spirit to overshadow us. We become silent, we dim the lights on the tree, we hold candles close and each other closer. It's as if we look upon our savior and finally mutter our own, "Let it be with me according to your word."

3. PEACE AROUND THE WORLD

One of my favorite things about the music from Tchaikovsky's *Nutcracker* ballet is the music from different cultures that comes together in celebration. Christmas is celebrated across the world, and it's so very interesting to see how different cultures and countries share the Nativity story. In America, many of us put trees in our living room, place lights on our homes, and hang stockings near the fireplace. People in Guatemala celebrate Christmas with tamales made of corn and rice or potatoes. People in Russia fast on Christmas Eve until they see the first star in the night sky. South Africans celebrate Christmas Eve with pudding and ice cream, as Christmas is a summer celebration. When the angel appears in the Bethlehem sky we hear, "I am bringing you good news of great joy for ALL the people." People all over the world on Christmas Eve sing "Silent Night" in their own language. This is when Christmas becomes truly beautiful. Our Christmas traditions and celebrations are personal and diverse, but they also bring us all together. Our traditions vary from family to family, house to house, congregation to congregation, nation to nation, and yet as Christians we are all reading the same story. It is indeed good news of great joy for all the people.

Advent is a peculiar season. It is a season of waiting for a Messiah we know has come. It is a time to meditate on the peace, hope, love, and joy Christ established, and yet we pray for these gifts to come into fruition. When we sing "Come, Thou Long-Expected Jesus," we sing not to herald the Christ-child so much as to announce that God's incarnational work of peace, hope, love, and joy which began in the humble manger continues today. One Christmas, I received a book of Italian arias, a collection of classical songs meant to train the voice. I can circle on the calendar when the gift was given, but it takes a lifetime to master the art of singing the songs well, and I'm not sure that it is something you ever quite finish. When we sing the songs of our faith about the coming Messiah, we acknowledge that God has already entered the world in the person of Jesus Christ, and yet we yearn and we groan with all of creation in waiting, hoping, and watching for God's work to come into fruition.

This is why we choose to start the Advent season with Peace. The Israelites had been exiled to Babylon in the sixth century, and their future, their story, and their identity as God's people appeared to be in jeopardy. As it says in Psalm 137:

> *By the rivers of Babylon—*
> *there we sat down and there we wept*
> *when we remembered Zion.*
> *On the willows there*
> *we hung up our harps.*
> *For there our captors*
> *asked us for songs,*
> *and our tormentors asked for mirth, saying,*
> *"Sing us one of the songs of Zion!"*
>
> *How could we sing the LORD's song*
> *in a foreign land?*
> *If I forget you, O Jerusalem,*
> *let my right hand wither!*
> *Let my tongue cling to the roof of my mouth,*
> *if I do not remember you,*
> *if I do not set Jerusalem*
> *above my highest joy.*
>
> *Psalm 137:1-6*

Jerusalem means "City of Peace," and the irony is that the Israelites were longing for anything but. The psalm ends with "Happy shall they be who pay you back what you have done to us," which is why God's first words proclaiming their return are "Comfort, O comfort my people." Not only does the Lord's word offer assurance of God's presence and a hope for the future, but it is also our example of how God desires us to respond in times of great tragedy and grief. Sometimes we have to say this holy phrase over and over again until it seeps deep into our souls past our all-too-human emotions. "Comfort, O comfort my people.... Speak tenderly to Jerusalem, and cry to her that she has served her term." God is speaking with the heavenly counsel for all the world to hear. Focus on Jerusalem, and surround my people with great love.

There is little mention of Babylon, only to say that Jerusalem has received double penalty through them. That great and terrible kingdom to the east offered punishment greater than what God had intended, but God calls the counsel and the world to set their eyes on the city of peace, so that violence might end, even though the exile was a stain on Israel's history. This is why Advent is important. We know that Christ has come, and Christ's life, suffering, death, and resurrection accomplished God's mission of revealing the kingdom of God on earth and in the everlasting, but Christ's work has not yet come to fruition within us.

Peace around the world doesn't happen overnight. Seeing the leaders of North and South Korea shaking hands over the Military Demarcation Line in April of 2018 offers a glimmer of hope that peace is possible. I pray that they continue to shake hands long after the cameras have gone. Peace is not simply the absence of conflict. A dictatorship is a relatively peaceful place because people are afraid to step out of line. Peace, or *Shalom*, is a wholeness and a healing. For example, when the skirmish between the Mouse King and the Nutcracker ended, peace did not begin until Drosselmeir healed the Nutcracker. And what a magnificent story it would be for Drosselmeir to have healed the Mouse King as well.

One way to begin offering *Shalom* to the world is through listening to and understanding those who aren't us. Last year my church's Advent series was called "Joyful All Ye Nations Rise," based on that great Charles Wesley hymn "Hark! The Herald Angels Sing." We created an Advent calendar for the congregation that offered twenty different Christmas traditions from around the world. For example, we learned that in South Korea, "Santa Grandfather" wears blue when he delivers presents to the children. In India, a banana tree may take the place of our traditional Christmas fir tree.

In my home, each night before putting the children to bed, we sat together as a family and talked about the traditions of whatever country was detailed on the Advent calendar that day. We opened Google maps so my kids could see where the countries were located. We searched Wikipedia and talked about the country's people, food, music, and culture. My children were absolutely astonished at how varied the different Christmas traditions were across the world. They became curious about our own traditions and why we celebrate the way we do. Talking about different Christmas traditions stirred in my children a great fascination about how we celebrate Christmas every year, as well as an understanding of how different and beautiful other traditions can be.

The Advent calendar itself was a long tan piece of cardstock, each day represented by a picture of a country's flag and a fun fact about how they celebrate Christmas in that area. We asked for families to tear away the strip for each country after discussing it together, but to save the pieces of the calendar. On Christmas Eve, we invited them to bring the tan strips of the calendar with them to worship, and place the strips, as if they were hay, in the manger in the chancel area. It became a beautiful picture to see the baby Jesus surrounded by the different countries of the world.

Christians across the world have unique understandings of how to celebrate Jesus' birth, but we are not as different as we might imagine. Our languages differ, the trees under which we place presents do not look the same, and the songs we sing on Christmas Eve have different melodies and tunes, but it all points to Christ. With Christ as our common bond, peace might not be a fairy tale after all.

4. LOVE AROUND THE WORLD

The character of the Nutcracker embodies the mystery of the Incarnation, God in the flesh in the person of Jesus Christ. God offers us the gift we need—himself, wrapped in the swaddling clothes of our humanity, born not in a palace, but among the poor. Was Clara dreaming? Did this really happen? It sounds impossible. Before the angel Gabriel departs from Mary, the angel says, "Nothing will be impossible with God" (Luke 1:37). That's an interesting way to talk about how God is moving in the world. You might think the angel would say that everything is possible with God, but the angel says "Nothing will be impossible." When the Gospel of John talks about Jesus' birth, we are reminded of creation: "In the beginning was the Word, and the Word was with God, and the Word was God" (John 1:1). In the beginning when God created the heavens and the earth, God looked upon the nothingness of the earth and filled the void with light, water, land, and life. God saw the nothing, and filled it with something. The angel doesn't say that everything is possible with God. I don't think we will ever see nutcrackers coming to life, mice twice our size, or dancing sugar plum fairies. Being a child of God means that nothing is impossible—the nothingness of darkness, the nothingness of fear and hopelessness. This is the nothing that cannot stand in the something of God's presence. Something will always outshine nothing.

Being a child of God means that nothing is impossible—the nothingness of darkness, the nothingness of fear and hopelessness. This is the nothing that cannot stand in the something of God's presence. Something will always outshine nothing.

One of the pictures we've placed prominently in our home is a sign that reads, "Where there is love, there are miracles." It is a reminder that instead of passively waiting for miracles to happen, we are called to actively share great love with one another and the world. When we grow in love of God and love of neighbor we begin to realize the miracles that were already happening. A friend of mine called me one evening to talk about his father. He recently heard that his dad was diagnosed with cancer and he was battling mixed emotions, as he and his father did not get along. It had been years since they had visited each other, and neither thought about the other as often as they should. Even though he held great resentment and regret about their relationship, he asked me to pray for a miracle. After offering a prayer inviting the Holy Spirit to make God's presence known, I asked my friend if he was willing to visit his father in the hospital. After a silence that seemed to last longer than it did, he agreed.

Over the next several months he sat by his father's bedside both at the hospital and in hospice. Initially the conversations were awkward and silent, with neither knowing exactly what to say. Over time, with great courage, honesty, and humility, they were able to begin forgiving each other for the pain that had torn their relationship apart. It certainly wasn't a happy time between the two, and not everything was reconciled between them. One could even argue that a healing miracle didn't happen, but something miraculous certainly moved between them. Healing doesn't always refer to our physical bodies. After the funeral, my friend mentioned that there was a peace about his father's passing. Although he couldn't forgive everything that had happened, he at least understood that his father was as imperfect as he was.

The miracle of Christmas isn't about gifts. The story of *The Nutcracker* actually isn't about the Nutcracker itself. Christmas and Advent is not a time of waiting for gifts; rather it is a time of waiting to recognize that the Giver is the gift. The gift is the invitation into God's story about how the human and the divine have come together in Christ and in the body of Christ, the church. In *God's Companions*, Sam Wells puts it this way:

> Whereas in earthly human friendship, intimate acquaintance invariably discloses unaddressed fragility, unresolved grief, and unquenched need, intimate knowledge of God discloses only awesome, sacrificial love.... Only God combines awe and intimacy in this way. The life of the kingdom is the unfolding of awe and intimacy on all creation. Meanwhile in earthly human friendship it is impossible to know everyone, still less to care or genuinely to love more than a limited number or range of people. Yet Jesus is the good shepherd, who knows all of his sheep and calls them each by name; he lays down his life for them. He is prepared to leave the great mass of them to seek and find just one. He has other sheep, "not of this fold," whom he knows just as well.... In other words, in the life of the kingdom it is possible to love all with the intensity

with which one might aspire on earth to love one; and that love and attention do not disclose deep flaws but evoke profound awe.[3]

God is the gift, and the gift is an invitation to participate in God's story—for God so loved the world that God became a part of it. Through Christ, God dwells within each of us. As the church, we are the place where God's story of love continues, the place where God's story of love is offered to the world. God is love, so when we learn to care, when we learn to share our gifts with the world, when we make room for those society has forgotten, or when we take the time to sit at the bedside of one we never thought we could forgive, that is when we experience the very heart of God. When we do these things, we create a place for God to dwell. It's the kind of environment that offers life. Like Drosselmeir bringing the Nutcracker to life, where there is love, there are miracles.

5. JOY AROUND THE WORLD

At the end of our story, Clara is seen peering out of the window, wondering if everything she has experienced is real. In a way, it's reminiscent of the day after Christmas. The presents have been opened, television programming seems blasphemously normal, and mom and dad get to experience learning what presents the children actually enjoy versus which presents they said they wanted but have not yet bothered to acknowledge. You might imagine that Clara's dreams continue to be filled with dancing with the Nutcracker during a grand evening ball. The Christmas story is a story about a dance as well. This story about Jesus' birth is a story about a God with a face, a God who has become incarnate so that we might know how to love God and love one another. This God with a face offers us a beautiful tension, at least as far as our minds are able to capture. When the infinite assumes the finite, when the almighty is emptied, when the divine puts on flesh, a dance ensues.

The day after Christmas, we sometimes live our lives as usual, quickly forgetting about the story we've learned. It's like giving your daughter an educational video game system that requires batteries, which means it is inevitably placed on a shelf until someone can remember to get batteries. You pray that during that period, your daughter has not forgotten about the gift altogether. Without batteries, it's as if you hadn't given the gift at all. Unless we live into the gift of the Christ child, it can be as if the gift hasn't been given.

One of my favorite Christmas Eve services was the first time I broke the rules. We all know there are few traditions more important than singing "Silent Night" by candlelight on Christmas Eve. Pastors may change many things about how her or his predecessor led worship, but adapting "Silent Night" at the end of the Christmas Eve worship service is dangerous territory. This particular year, we ended our worship service with David Crowder's version of the song. It began with our lead guitar playing solo on his acoustic instrument, and over the course of the song the other band members joined in; the tempo sped up gradually, and the beat began to change. At the end of the song, the band played a full-out two-step that made you want to dance out of the sanctuary and into the world. It may have been a silent night, but it wasn't silent for long.

I'd be lying if I said the change was well-accepted, but I still assert that playing a two-step is the perfect way to end a Christmas Eve service. That simple silent night thousands of years ago started a revolution across the world. Singing a two-step reminded us that the human and the divine came together in the person of Jesus

Christ, leading us in a dance with God ushering in the joy of salvation coming into the world.

Christmas is only the beginning. Jesus' first word in the Gospel of Luke is "Why." "Why were you searching for me?" he says to his mother after she has found him in the Temple. In Matthew's Gospel, Jesus first says, "Let it be," speaking to John, who wonders why it is he who is supposed to do the baptizing. "Let it be." Does that not remind you of creation? When we put these two Gospels together we see the dance happening within Jesus. God's divinity is shining through when Jesus first speaks in Matthew, and in Luke, Jesus speaks the most human word of all, "Why."

There is no other word about which more ink has been spilled. At the end of Luke's Gospel after the Resurrection, Jesus appears to his disciples and says, "'These are my words that I spoke to you while I was still with you—that everything written about me in the Law of Moses, the prophets, and the psalms must be fulfilled.' Then he opened their minds to understand the scriptures." Jesus begins with a human "why," and then ends with a divine unlocking of mystery. The dance is complete, and Jesus sends the disciples forth to teach the world how to move with the Holy Spirit.

Jesus takes on our human questioning and redeems it with a holy and resurrected answer of love. The dance between the human and the divine is complete in the person of Jesus, and the blessing is that God invites us to be partners in this dance. One year, on the last Sunday of Advent, we lit the candle of Joy on our home Advent wreath. I asked my daughter what "Joy" meant to her. She said, "It means happy enough to dance."

It is not enough to remember the dance, like Clara staring out of the window hoping that her story was true. Only watching the dance is like forgetting the batteries or leaving Jesus in the sanctuary on the day after Christmas. We are called to dance in the world with steps of justice, humility as our partner, and love playing the tune. It is no mistake that *The Nutcracker* ends with a celebration where people from all over the world are welcome, the Mouse King is nowhere to be found, and Drosselmeir is standing in the background admiring what he seems to have created.

It is not enough to remember the dance, like Clara staring out of the window hoping that her story was true. Only watching the dance is like forgetting the batteries or leaving Jesus in the sanctuary on the day after Christmas. We are called to dance in the world with steps of justice, humility as our partner, and love playing the tune.

Christmas is the day that God was born in the world in the person of Jesus Christ. Jesus came so that we might be redeemed (bought back) and justified (set right) so that people of every nation, creed, color, and status might dance together for the transformation of the world. Christ's work is not about the gifts, but about the giver. Our work is not about receiving as much as it is about giving. Jesus was born in Bethlehem, the "House of Bread," so that Christ might be our nourishment for the journey we call life. Jesus was raised in Nazareth, or "New Shoot," because the life he offers to us and our neighbors is renewed every day by the power of God's Holy Spirit. Jesus was arrested and crucified in Jerusalem, the "City of Peace," so that we might no longer teach and learn war, making all cities yearn for the peace it offers. Through a twelve-year-old's imagination, a godfather's great love, the defeat of a mouse king, and the gift of a nutcracker who becomes real, we discover the beauty of God's greatest gift to us—the gift of Jesus.

Devotion

THE STORY CONTINUES

And the Word became flesh and lived among us, and we have seen his glory, the glory as of a father's only son, full of grace and truth.

John 1:14

After the Nutcracker is killed by the Mouse King and resurrected by Clara's godfather, Drosselmeir, he becomes a real, flesh-and-blood prince. He then takes Clara back to his kingdom, where they are greeted by people from all over the world who are celebrating their arrival. It's a magnificent and joyful ending to a story that began with much waiting, uncertainty, and a gift that Clara didn't ask for or even think that she needed.

The parallel for us is profound. Jesus, who is the Word that became flesh and made his dwelling among us, certainly is the gift we need from God; but he may not always be the gift we *want* from God. Think about it. On the one hand, Jesus gives us everything; he is the Source of all that we need and the very way that leads to life. On the other hand, he asks something of us. Jesus calls us to give generously, serve those in need, deny ourselves, live obediently and sacrificially, and love our enemies. Sometimes that may not seem to be what we want. We prefer comfort, success, and prosperity over humility, struggle, and sacrifice. But following Jesus is not about our gain but about God's grace. When we remember God's boundless grace toward us, we want to share that grace with others. Jesus may not always seem like the gift we want, but he certainly is the gift we need.

As we've made our way through the Advent season, we've known all along that this great gift of God, Jesus, has already come. Christ's life, death, and resurrection accomplished the divine rescue mission—revealing God's heart of love and the Kingdom, both here on earth and still to come. Yet God's work is also ongoing—within our world and within each of us. We are works in progress, "going on to perfection" as John Wesley put it. The story isn't over.

When we accept the invitation to participate in God's ongoing work, sharing our gifts and offering God's love, the story continues in us and through us, conforming us to the image of Christ and transforming the world around us. And like Drosselmeir bringing the Nutcracker to life, the miracle of Christmas is greater than anything we ever could have imagined.

Most generous God, I am so grateful for the unsurpassed gift of Jesus, who took on flesh for my sake and the sake of the world. Thank you for your boundless grace—and the opportunity to share your grace and love with others. Continue your story in and through me, not only at Christmas but every day of the year. Amen.

Epilogue

When is a story complete? When is an experience finally over? Sometimes it's easy to tell. The narrator says they live happily ever after, the curtain closes, the audience stands in ovation, and we all leave the theater. Or consider the beauty of a joke. In south Louisiana we like to tell "Boudreaux and Thibodeaux" jokes.

Boudreaux and Thibodeaux went fishing early one morning, and Thibodeaux noticed that Boudreaux was sipping something from a strange container.

"What is that?" Thibodeaux asked.

"It's a thermos. It keeps hot things hot and cold things cold. See, I'm drinking coffee, and it's still warm," Boudreaux replied.

"I see," said Thibodeaux.

The next week Boudreaux and Thibodeaux went to a local catfish fry downtown for lunch, and Thibodeaux noticed Boudreaux again had a thermos.

"Why are you drinking coffee in the middle of the day?" Thibodeaux asked.

"It's iced tea," Boudreaux replied.

"Why do you want your iced tea to get hot?" Thibodeaux asked.

"It's not," said Boudreaux. "The thermos keeps hot things hot and cold things cold. See, there's still ice in my tea."

"I see," said Thibodeaux.

The next week Boudreaux and Thibodeaux went to a football game, and Thibodeaux was excited to show Boudreaux his brand-new thermos.

"I see you got you a new thermos."

"That's right! It keeps hot things hot and cold things cold!"

"Whatcha drinkin'?"

"Here, take a sip."

Boudreaux took a long gulp from Thibodeaux's thermos, quickly spitting out the disgusting taste in his mouth.

"This is terrible! What did you put in your thermos?"

"Chicken soup and ice cream…"[1]

I'm not sure a joke can exist without a definitive ending or punch line. We miss the point of the joke if we become concerned with what our friends Boudreaux and Thibodeaux are doing the next week, or whether their favorite team won the football game, or what they will be having for dinner (unless that's another joke just waiting to happen). The curtain has to close on the story, or we miss the point altogether. *The Nutcracker* has a definitive beginning, and in one sense, it has to. You open the book to read the short story, you go to the theater to see the curtain rise, or you log in to a streaming service to listen to Tchaikovsky's music. You are introduced to Clara and her dreams, you read with curiosity when Drosselmeir surprisingly enters the story, and you wonder what might happen when the Nutcracker and the Mouse King are locked in a duel. *The Nutcracker* also has a definitive ending. Clara wakes up at the end of the story knowing that all she has experienced was a dream, but it is a dream that she will remember for years to come. There comes a time when the ballet is over, you read "the end," or the music is finished.

Sometimes things end before they even get going. For many years Christmas has fallen into this category for me. We spend months preparing, planning, making lists and checking them twice. The benediction at the Christmas Eve service feels like an ending of sorts. The church staff finally exhales, looking forward to the office being closed the next day, we open presents the next morning and plan our traveling, and my calendar turns to start thinking about our big January worship series. Christmas Eve concludes the twelve days of Christmas. I know that Christmas Eve is a prelude to the main event, but sometimes it feels like I'm in the audience and after the orchestra plays the overture, I gather my things and head home.

Have you had a similar experience? We clergy tend to fall into two categories when it comes to Advent and Christmas: Liturgical Purists and Cultural Coordinators (and maybe there's an unfortunate third category of those who don't plan at all). On the polar ends of the divide, the purists sing only Advent hymns in the weeks prior to Christmas, they lift up Old Testament prophesies that point to Christ, and "Joy to the World" is only offered on Christ the King Sunday (the Sunday before Advent) because that was the original intent of the song. The Cultural Coordinators have little problem singing "The First Noel" on the first Sunday of Advent. With there being only one Sunday in the actual liturgical season of Christmas, they broaden the timeline to incorporate Advent and Christmas as a single, celebratory time.

I can't say which group is more correct in their handling of announcing Christ's birth other than to recognize that the liturgical calendar itself is a cultural expression of the Christian faith (meaning that Scripture doesn't dictate when the liturgical seasons should be), and that one might want to wait to sing "Away in a Manger" until Jesus is actually in the manger. If you've ever read any of my other books you may begin to realize that I like to both honor and question polar reactions to any kind of divide (with some exceptions).

With that said, it is important to recognize that Christmas is more than the Christmas Eve service. The liturgical calendar is more than a schedule. It is a common heartbeat that Christians across the globe all share together. We begin the Christian year with Advent, a holy waiting for God-made-flesh to enter into creation. After a silent night huddled around a manger, we spend twelve days celebrating and reflecting on what this birth means. We take the time to ponder with Mary as she hears Simeon say when Jesus is presented at the Temple, "This child is destined for the falling and rising of many in Israel, and to be a sign that will be opposed so that the inner thoughts of many will be revealed—and a sword will pierce your own soul too" (Luke 2:34-35).

It isn't long before the liturgical calendar unapologetically turns to the season of Epiphany. We experience thirty or so years of Jesus' life from one Sunday to the next. Epiphany is a season to marvel over what God is doing in the world. We hear stories of Jesus' healings and miraculous voices from heaven calling us to listen to God's beloved son. Marveling at God's holiness and grandeur then gives way to inner reflection on our own finitude and frailty as we turn to the season of Lent. Forty days of preparation and humility, in step with Jesus' forty days in the wilderness, offers our soul time to recognize the great passion of grace and love God has for the world, revealed through Christ's broken body and blood outpoured.

Then lilies adorn the altar/table, trumpets welcome us into the sanctuary, and we celebrate and give thanks that death has lost its sting. Easter is the great feast of our faith, the affirmation that God's word is true. Our story will forever continue in abundant, resurrection life. Just when you think the story has reached its conclusion, God surprises us with Pentecost. The disciples were all gathered in one place, and suddenly there was a sound like the rush of a violent wind. The Holy Spirit was poured out upon the disciples, and something like fire remained with them. The disciples began offering the word of God, and people from every nation who had gathered in Jerusalem that day heard God in a language they could recognize.

For most of the year we rest in this fire-filled time of the church, and this makes great sense. When the Holy Spirit moves among us, we hear God in a language we can understand. This Pentecost story is one of the reasons why I love writing about the intersection between Christ and culture. God used the established culture of language to share a new, unfiltered communion with God's people. This story would be altogether different if the Holy Spirit was speaking a new, spiritual language that those who gathered in Jerusalem had to learn, but that's not the story we've been given. In other words, in what ways is God already speaking to us of which we are unaware? Language is a way we express how we make sense of the world. From culture to culture, household to household, and nation to nation, language holds within its vowels and consonants a nuanced picture of its spoken community. Instead of throwing away this established cultural nuance, God chose to take hold of it and use it for the building of God's kingdom.

This Kingdom finds its liturgical culmination in Christ the King Sunday at the end of the Christian year. We lift our hands high to offer praise to Christ, who sits at God's right hand. Christ is our judge, our savior, and our companion on the way that leads to life. Nothing can separate us from this glorious love, and we end our worshipful year recognizing that all things have been reconciled through Christ. All things have been reconciled—even you and me.

Does that mean our story is finished? I hope not. When we think of a story like *The Nutcracker*, there is a definitive time when the story is over, but the fact that the story has been told and retold for over a hundred years means that the story isn't over until it is forgotten. The language I best understand is music. With music there is a definitive beginning and an ending. During worship, when it makes sense, I love to end a song without getting back to the tonic, the home pitch around which the song is centered.

Seemingly instinctively, we are left uneasy as if there's more to come. It's like if someone says, "Tomorrow, I would like you to…" You're still waiting for what comes next. I hope worship always feels like this. I hope every time you exit the sanctuary you are left with both a fulfillment of God's presence and a desire to see what God has in store for you. At the very least, if a song does find its home tone at the end, I hope it won't be the last time you ever sing.

Following Christ the King Sunday, the very next Sunday we gather in the sanctuary for the first Sunday of Advent to start the story all over again. I wonder if it's most appropriate for every day to resonate with the liturgical year? When we rise in the morning we see the day anew, as we invite Christ into our lives. We marvel at the mystery of it all, giving thanks for what we have discovered about ourselves and the world, and then trusting that all things work for the glory of God when pondering the things we don't know. Reveling in this mystery leads us to humbly seek the presence of God within ourselves, investigating what we need to give up or what we need to take on to prepare ourselves to carry the cross with Christ on our daily journey. But the cross we carry is surrounded by a promise of life, so that in losing our lives we might find them. Knowing that our story ends with life, we have the courage to speak and share the language we best understand for the glory of God to all that we might meet throughout the day. Finally, before we close our eyes for rest, we recognize, remember, and give thanks that we rest under the rule of a compassionate and graceful savior.

Is it wrong to sing a Christmas hymn or two during Advent? Is it inappropriate to mention mystery during Lent and humility during Epiphany? Is it somehow inappropriate to listen to *The*

Nutcracker in the spring? Disney's *Fantasia* uses Tchaikovsky's music without referencing *The Nutcracker* or Christmas. How does that change the music's meaning? Music is simply a graph of pitch verses time. If you place the pitches in a different order (plotting them differently in time) then you come out with a different melody. There's a chance you might change the tune itself, sometimes with terrible consequences. But this doesn't mean you can't add accents or dynamics, coloring a chord here and there with a bluesy seventh or adding tension with competing pitches. The liturgical calendar is important for ordering our lives together, but the calendar is never more important than the content found within. Of course, interpretation is a key component with instrumental music. Without words to guide the pictures you form in your mind, meaning is more subjective than we might care to admit.

So, I hope in the days after Christmas Eve and into the new year the Christmas decorations are still up. At first blush it might look like you forgot to change out the visuals. Once Christmas Eve has passed, the rest of the world will seem to have moved on. On the one hand, the calendar will change, which will give your fellow worshipers a sense of a new beginning, but on the other hand, the church is saying, "Hold on. Don't forget." It's not that Jesus is the reason for the season; it's that Jesus *is*. As you turn the page into a new year, remember to continue to live in hope, fight the good fight for peace, learn to love, and be filled with joy. The Giver is the gift and that gift is alive today.

Christianity is filled with holy tension. When we live in a kingdom that is here but not yet, when we live in a time between Christ's resurrection and the end when heaven and earth will be one, we live in the midst of tension. In chapter 2 of Ephesians, the Apostle Paul talks about how powerful God is in the person of Jesus and how Jesus abolishes hostility through the cross, yet Paul is writing this letter from jail. It doesn't look good. In a way, Paul is saying, "I know how this looks, but have hope that God is continuing to reveal a mystery." There is a tension in God's story. It's like someone walking into a sanctuary in which the tree is still up and we say, "I know how this looks, but hold on, let me explain."

Paul talks about a mystery, and the mystery is that God is bringing people together in Christ. Ephesians says, "In former generations this mystery was not made known to humankind, as it has now been revealed to his holy apostles and prophets by the Spirit; that is, the Gentiles have become fellow heirs, members of the same body, and sharers in the promise in Christ Jesus through the gospel" (Ephesians 3:5-6). God is bringing people together, God is fulfilling an ancient promise, and I have a notion of how this will play out: the stories at the end will probably not be stories of grace, love, and mercy, but will have hope that the tension we see in the world, the tension which makes the mystery of this coming year difficult to bear, will be redeemed through Christ and the body of Christ working together.

The author of Ephesians says, "This was in accordance with the eternal purpose that he has carried out in Christ Jesus our Lord, in whom we have access to God in boldness and confidence through faith in him" (Ephesians 3:11-12).We have a role to play in God's unfolding mystery. We should be bold and confident in our faith, and put our faith into practice in the world.

I know what it looks like. The Christmas decorations are still up but the calendar has turned to a new year. We come to sit in the uncomfortable tension of a world that has come but has not yet come into fruition. We hang on to the story of Emmanuel—God is with us—just a beat longer than the world expects so that we can proclaim that we are not alone, that no one is alone. I know what it looks like. It looks like a community ready to be used by God to change the world.

I love how Revelation, the last book of the Bible, begins with "Grace to you and peace from him who is and who was and who is to come…" (Revelation 1:4b). When we worship and serve a God who is (living in our present), who was (redeeming our past), and who is to come (leading us into a hopeful future), our story is never complete until God decides to make the new heaven and new earth one at the end of all things. It may seem that the curtain has fallen, and the actors have taken a bow, but the story continues. It's true that a good joke or a piece of music has a definitive beginning and ending, but the story continues when a new audience fills the auditorium, or a new group is ready for a good laugh.

Who in your community needs to hear this story? Who will bless you with fresh eyes and ears to hear the magnificent story of God's grace? What language might you use to tell God's story? Is your language music or math, construction or poetry, sports or dance? If Pentecost teaches us anything, it is that God can use the language you already know to offer the world a good word. Don't feel you need to start with Advent. Sometimes our relationship with God begins with mystery or a newly found humility. Sometimes our first word from God is forgiveness or power. If every day can be a liturgical season in and of itself, it doesn't matter where you belong, as long as you keep going. May every day be a journey through a newness of life, revealing through God's mystery a deep dive into self-reflection, thanksgiving for abundant life, a call to action to share God's story, and the trust and assurance that God will always be our God. Even though you close the cover of *The Nutcracker* and they all live happily ever after, the story is never finished until we stop sharing it. May we continue to share God's story until we breathe our last.

Acknowledgments

I am honored and humbled to share this study with you, but this study would not have happened without some very special people. I first have to thank my wife, Christie, and my amazing kids Isabelle, Annaleigh, Cecilia, and Robert for sharing me with the ministry in general and this study in particular.

I thank Rev. Ken Irby for opening his home and ministry to my family. Thank you, Dr. James C. Howell, for continuing to be an inspiration. I also thank Rev. Dr. Sam Wells for shaping how I see the world. I must acknowledge the support of my colleagues in the Louisiana Conference of The United Methodist Church and the grace I have received from the churches I have served. I especially want to thank Asbury United Methodist Church for offering me the grace and space to work on this study.

I am always so thankful to Abingdon Press for offering me the opportunity to share the gospel through studies. To the team: Susan Salley, Alan Vermilye, Tim Cobb, Maria Mayo, Lauren Arieux, and Angie Cason. I especially want to thank Ron Kidd. Enjoy your retirement, brother! Hope to see you in Epcot one of these days!

THE RAWLE BALLERINAS

Annaleigh Rawle
at age 8 (2017)

Cecilia Rawle
at age 4 (2017)

*This is a drawing of Clara that
Isabelle (11 yrs old) created on the iPad.*

Notes

Chapter Two
1. "The Baptismal Covenant I," in *The United Methodist Hymnal* (Nashville: The United Methodist Publishing House, 1989), 34.
2. Matthew 9:1-8; Mark 2:1-12; Luke 5:17-26.
3. James Nicholson, "The Lord Is My Light," in *Christ in Song Hymnal* (London: F.E. Belden, 1900), 528.

Chapter Three
1. Eleanor Farjeon, "People, Look East," in *The United Methodist Hymnal* (Nashville: The United Methodist Publishing House, 1989), 202.

Chapter Four
1. "A Service of Word and Table I," in *The United Methodist Hymnal,* (Nashville: The United Methodist Publishing House, 1989), 8.
2. Ibid.
3. Samuel Wells, *God's Companions: Reimagining Christian Ethics* (Maiden, MA: Blackwell 2006), page 41.

Epilogue
1. Origin unknown.